Louise Etheridge was born in Bradford-on-Avon, which is not Bradford. She was educated in Kent and Scotland and studied at Edinburgh University where she learned things that make her good in a pub quiz. After a "portfolio" career in which she enjoyed numbers, helped to build satellites and forced people to learn to read, she gave it all up for a life of penury as a writer, poet and lyricist. *Happy Stories for Busy People* is her first collection of short stories and will probably be her last.

Happy Stories
for Busy People

Louise Etheridge

An Angry Hen Press book

First published by Angry Hen Press, November 2012

This edition December 2015

The legal stuff:

ISBN: 978-0-9574315-3-9

www.louiseetheridge.com

louise@louiseetheridge.com

CONTENTS

1 KATRINA TELLS A LIE

This is a story about Katrina and what happened the day she told a lie.

To you or me, lying might come quite easily. I'm sure one of us has said, "The cheque's in the post," or "Darling, of course I love you," or even, "Officer, this man was already dead when I found him." If so, shame on us!

But Katrina wasn't like us. She had a strict regard for truth. Honesty was her middle name. Really, it was — her parents christened her Katrina Honesty, because they too had a strict regard for truth.

Once, when she was seven years old and sitting down to tea with her mum and dad, she made the mistake of asking where babies came from. And because her mum and dad had a strict regard for truth, they didn't mention gooseberry bushes or the stork or even how mummy and daddy had a special hug, like my friend Glenda says to Dirk and Regina when they ask about this kind of thing. Instead, they launched into a description of the whole gory process, complete with hand gestures, the bolder elements of kabuki theatre and even diagrams drawn on the tablecloth in tomato ketchup. Queasy but unbowed,

Katrina pushed away her plate of toad in the hole and pondered why the truth was sometimes unpleasant.

She also wondered why telling the truth seemed to get her into trouble. When Katrina was 14, her Aunt Edith came to stay, wearing a particularly vile hat. Aunt Edith said, "Do you like my hat, Katrina?"

"Not really. It looks like a pigeon with dermatitis. Is it one?" said Katrina, wondering how Aunt Edith had caught it and persuaded it to sit on her head, all the way from Pinner. Aunt Edith turned an interesting shade of red. Artists would have called it vermillion and ten minutes later Katrina was packed upstairs to bed with absolutely no tea.

"What did I do wrong?" mused Katrina, "I only told the truth."

At university she was too honest for boyfriends. Darren really liked her and once said, "Do you love me, Katrina?"

"No," said Katrina, although it made her sad to say so.

"Oh." Darren looked rather hurt. "I was rather hoping for a better answer," he said.

"Would you prefer a lie?" asked Katrina.

"Well, yes, actually, I would."

"But why?"

"Because it feels better than the truth."

Katrina couldn't understand. "But it's not true! How can pretend feel better than real?"

Darren shrugged and thought that perhaps Caroline Crenshaw in Linguistics might be more his type.

Katrina did try having lots of boyfriends for a term, just to see if it were more honest. One of her lovers took her in his arms, and said, "Katrina, am I the first man ever to make love to you?"

"You might be," Katrina said, "your face seems familiar."

Love went pear-shaped from then on.

After university she found a job teaching in an infant

school. She liked the fact that little children and honesty went together very well. Children didn't seem to mind the truth, except during art. Alfie, her brightest and best-behaved child, ran up to her waving a piece of paper.

"Miss, Miss, I've finished!" he said breathlessly, pink with pleasure and excited about his glorious picture. "I bet Miss will love it," he thought.

"Look at my picture, Miss!"

"Alfie, very nice. Yes, very nice. But what's this here?"

"It's the sky, Miss."

"But it's green!"

"Yes, Miss. I thought it would be nice to be green. Sometimes it feels green."

"Oh. And what's this?" asked Katrina, pointing to some blue splodges.

"It's the trees, Miss. Like the ones in the playing field."

Katrina said, quite kindly, "But these are blue. Since when are trees blue? And, oh, look, Alfie, the sun definitely does not have a face."

Alfie's own face fell. "Well, he feels smiley when he is out..." and he tailed off.

"That really is as may be, but it's not true," Katrina said briskly. "Can you do it again, please, properly, this time?"

"Oh, all right, Miss." Alfie walked slowly back to his table.

The other teachers liked Katrina but soon learned never to ask her whether their bums looked big in anything. Every day was the same for Katrina. She got up early, had her breakfast, walked to school, taught class, walked back home, made her tea and ate it while watching the telly. And then she went to bed.

You might survive doing this for one day a week, or even two days or three. I know some resilient people who do the same thing every day for four days a week. But Katrina did this for five days a week. And at the weekends she was content with her puzzles and her jigsaws, and pottering around her pretty garden, and knitting egg cosies, or jackets for Mrs Deans-next-door's Westie, Rupert. Sometimes she even chatted with Mrs Deans-next-door over the garden fence, but more often she chatted to nobody.

Her life repeated its daily routine for 15 years and Katrina was content. When I say she was content, that might have been a tiny lie. This story is about lies, after all. Katrina was mostly content, but sometimes she felt a little sliver of a silver flame inside, a flame that wanted to be heard, be felt, be seen, and be known. She knew she was a happy and friendly person. She wanted people to know her. She wanted to fit in.

One amazing day she was flicking through one of the stodgy papers that were squished through her letterbox at the weekends, and saw something in the shiny colour supplement – that's the slippery part that you secretly sniff and then regret it – something that made her sit bolt upright, and which for a brisk second launched airborne a fruit scone complete with butter and quince preserve. What Katrina had seen to make her lose her scone was an advert for a summer school. As she eagerly read the advert she learned that a summer school was a place where you stayed for a week and could learn to do almost anything you liked. She gasped at the choices. If she wanted, she could paint pictures of bare people or dowse ancient monuments or make puppet monsters or abseil from bridges or throw pots or do stand-up or learn about rodents. Because she had always liked art, she really fancied doing some drawing of people, even if they had clothes on. And when the brochure arrived everyone looked happy and friendly. At last she would fit in. She sent off her cheque and six weeks later she was there.

The first morning at summer school, she walked into the dining hall. Nervously she chose her breakfast — toast and butter, nothing too fiddly that she might drop on her clean top — and looked around the room. Who could she talk to? Among the buzz and chatter of the groups of people around the tables, she saw a woman on her own.

"She looks a bit lonely. I'll go and sit with her," thought Katrina.

As she approached, the woman looked up but didn't speak. Or smile.

"May I sit here? Aren't these trays heavy!" began Katrina, hoping that a warm pleasantry and engaging smile might be a good start. She was wrong.

"Well, you shouldn't eat so much," said the woman, whose pursed lips and gooseberry eyes frightened Katrina so much that she was just about to turn away and find somewhere by herself when the woman said,"Oh, very well. Sit down. No, not there. I'm saving that seat for my friend."

Katrina was brought up to be polite and instead of saying something like, "How ill-bred you are!" or "That is very kind but I have just remembered I must take my anti-psychotic tablets," or even "I curse you a thousand times and may your legs drop off in the night," she sat down.

What's your name?" barked the woman.

"Katrina."

"What kind of silly name is that? What's wrong with Katherine?"

"Well, er, it's not my name."

"Why don't you have a good proper English name, like mine? I'm Margaret. You look like you have to work. What do you do?"

"I'm an infant school teacher."

"How ordinary."

Katrina wasn't used to abrupt rudeness and didn't know what to say, so she said nothing. She scraped some butter on to her toast and took a bite. She usually loved toast and butter but things weren't going to plan. Everyone was supposed to be friendly, that's what the pictures on the brochure said.

Then she felt something coming her way, something

big. A shadow fell over her toast and then she heard a big loud scary voice say, "What ho, Margaret!"

"Ah, Olivia, there you are. Do sit here; I saved it especially for you."

Katrina half turned, the chair next to her scraped out, and Olivia sat down. If you ever were to see a sofa-sized overstuffed cushion in a floral kaftan eating with its mouth open, that would be Olivia.

"Excellent sausages this morning," began Olivia. "Who's this?" She stabbed her finger at Katrina.

"Oh, no one," Margaret said. "Tell me, darling, what are you covering in Art Appreciation this year?"

"The Impressionists, of course."

Katrina knew lots about the Impressionists. Hadn't she spent whole weekends on her own, lost for words in online art galleries, revelling in Renoir, Bazille and Sisley? Hoping to be included, she said "I love the Impressionists. They are the ones that paint it like it isn't and yet such open composition, such bold brush strokes and…"

"Like it isn't? How absurd! Who is this, Margaret?" squealed Olivia with a gasping guffaw.

"Karenza. Funny foreign girl. She's a teacher, so she can't do anything."

"But…," said Katrina.

"She doesn't know much, either!"

"That's not…."

"What do they teach teachers these days? No wonder the youth of today have brains like an overripe Brie! Now when I was a girl…," started Olivia.

"Olivia, how is that wonderful art tutor of yours?" said Margaret.

"Oh, Sebastian is absolutely stunning, as usual. All of us adore him."

Turning away from Katrina they giggled together like conspiratorial teenagers. Katrina was the outsider again. Her eyes felt blurry with tears as she looked down at the butter congealing on her cold toast.

(There is a big lie coming up. Look away now if you are morally upmarket.)

And then something deep inside Katrina snapped. She decided that, just this once, just this one time, she was going to tell a big, fat, luscious, beautiful, juicy lie.

She turned to face them squarely, like people do when they are going to say something bold and interesting and perhaps not without controversy. Something in her manner made them look at her. Katrina said, slowly and deliberately. "Sebastian is stunning, isn't he? I know him very well. Very well indeed."

Margaret and Olivia frowned.

"How on earth could you know Sebastian? You haven't even been to summer school! You don't know anything about art!" Margaret said.

"I do know about art. And I tell you why I know a lot about art. You see," said Katrina, trying a dramatic pause, "Sebastian is my lover."

If Katrina Tells a Lie had been a cartoon on television you would have seen Margaret and Olivia's jaws extend at the hinges and hit the table with a smack. But this is a written-down story so you will have to imagine that that would have been the effect had their jaws had that capability.

"Your lover!" squealed Margaret.

"Your lover!" squeaked Olivia.

"Yes," said Katrina, with what she hoped was a faraway, yearning gaze, "I've tried to break it off with him. Every day he begs me, "Please, Katrina, I can't live without you." And of course, I can't live without him."

"Katrina! But he's the most gorgeous thing. You little minx!"

Margaret and Olivia looked at her with admiring eyes. They drew their chairs up a little closer to her. Katrina felt triumphant. She had their attention and their respect. Then Olivia cocked her flabby head and said,

"Does his wife know?"

His wife? Katrina's brain raced. She'd forgotten about

wives.

"No," she said, "Yvette doesn't suspect a thing."

"But I thought his wife is called Doris!"

Katrina's brain raced even faster.

"Oh, she is called Doris, certainly. Yvette is her middle name. She's half French, of course. But Sebastian will never call her that. He hates the French."

Olivia gasped. "But he lives for French art! Monet, Manet, Delacroix…they are his raison d'être!"

Katrina thought even more quickly but, underneath the near panic and mental athletics, she began to enjoy herself.

"But can't you see that's the most perfect ploy?" she said. "To pretend to love the thing you hate most? My Sebastian is so clever."

"Yes," mused Margaret, "I see it now. That's why he holidays in the Dordogne every year; to visit Yvette's parents. How that must torment him."

Olivia cleared her throat, her chin fat wobbling with anticipation, and said, "What I'd like to know, well, what everyone would like to know is...what's he like in bed?" She swirled the words around her mouth like a tasty Merlot, the kind you drink when you've just got back from a very trying day at work and you haven't even taken your coat off.

"Oh dear God," thought Katrina, "imaginary shenanigans with a man I've never met isn't really what I want to discuss." But she couldn't backtrack now. And what would Sebastian be like, anyway? She grasped for adjectives. Olivia and Margaret were looking at her.

"He's very… bendy," she announced.

Bendy. Was that all she could come up with? Katrina was horrified at herself. Why not passionate? Romantic, why not that? Even kinky would be a little risqué and therefore perfectly acceptable. But bendy?

There was a puzzled silence. Then Margaret said, "But doesn't his wooden leg give you problems?"

"His wooden leg?" said Katrina. She was starting to

regret picking Sebastian as an object of fraudulence. But gamely she carried on. "Not at all," she said. "It adds to the passion. He gets me to dress up like a badger and nibble on it."

It was then that she thought the game was up. How could they possibly believe her story? Hardly anyone she knew believed that dressing as any stripy native wildlife was in the least bit naughty. But Margaret was entranced.

"How erotic! How superbly British. I envy you, Katrina. And your name is so delightful. Scots, isn't it? I do so love the Trossachs." Margaret laid a reptilian claw on Katrina's arm.

"It must have been awful for him, losing his leg in that terrible accident," sighed Olivia.

"Yes, the threshing machine," said Katrina, taking a plunge.

"I thought he was run over!" exclaimed Margaret.

"Certainly he was run over," agreed Katrina "by a threshing machine. Driven by a Frenchman. That's why he hates the French!"

It was all falling into place. She couldn't stop now. Everything she had got wrong she had made gloriously right.

(It's at this stage that people who lie get a little overconfident. You can tell because they sit back in their chairs, gaze into the middle distance with a slight frown as if recalling the incident only too clearly. Be careful of people you see doing this, as they are lying to you.)

"Where did you and Sebastian meet?" asked Olivia.

"At St Chuffing's Hospital – the neurosurgery place in London. I was exhausted. I'd been operating on a man's brain for nine hours..." Katrina tailed off, gazing into the middle distance with a slight frown (see above).

"I thought you said you were an infant teacher!"

"I am, I am. I teach… er… brain surgery. Anyway, it was love at first sight. We were in the hospital canteen and we both reached for the same almond slice...."

"But he has a terrible nut allergy!" gasped Margaret.

9

"One bite of an almond slice would kill him! Olivia, remember that unfortunate incident with the brazil nut parfait at the Master's Ball?"

"Good Lord, yes. They were still mopping up the custard a week later. But I suppose being a brain surgeon you could have dealt with any medical emergency," said Olivia.

Katrina didn't want to go down that road. No amount of watching Casualty would make her a convincing liar on medical issues. "Do you know, I think it may actually have been a French Fancy."

"But he hates the French!"

"Damn the French!" Katrina thought, and said, "Yes, but don't you see? He was so smitten with me that he wouldn't even have noticed if he'd picked up a cursèd be-nutted cakelet that to him meant certain death or a bun to do with the French whom he despises. Or any old cake really; that's not the point. As soon as I gazed into his beautiful blue eyes…."

"Doesn't he have brown eyes?"

Ah. Katrina sat forward abruptly, not so confident now. She delved deep into her knowledge bank of real medical conditions and found it sadly wanting. But what was not wanting was her imagination, fully alive to the ways out of traps she had flung at herself. With a sudden glow of guilty pleasure, she realised that she was very good at lying.

"Oh yes, he has lovely brown eyes now," she agreed. "Very El Greco. But when we first met, his eyes were as blue as your lovely pleated skirt, Margaret. Losing his leg affected his eye colour. He's developed a humectal chondroplasmia in his lower right vibula, and that of course changed his eye colour from brown to blue."

"Blue to brown," corrected Margaret.

"Yes, that's it. It's all due to the pressure of the aqueous mandustible on the lesser optic squandula. It's very common in threshing machine accidents, especially on the continent."

Katrina winced. Surely she'd be found out now. But, no. They were buying it.

"But what on earth was Sebastian doing in hospital? He always prides himself on how healthy he is," said Margaret. "Despite his leg, he performs a full salutation of yoga on the lawn before breakfast. We all watch him. His feathered peacock is a joy to behold."

"Yes, he's very fit," agreed Katrina, "but he wasn't at hospital for him. He was there because Yvette, I mean Doris, was giving birth to their baby."

Olivia looked puzzled and, leaning back to give her tummies more room, said, "But Sebastian and Doris are childless. He told me that they had been trying for a baby for years, and my view is that her uterus was too dry and crispy to bear fruit. How like the French to ruin an Englishman's dream."

"Oh dear," thought Katrina, but ploughed manfully on. "Yes, of course, he would say that. He told me he couldn't bear to embarrass Doris. She did have the baby but she couldn't handle motherhood so the baby was adopted by a tribe of wandering chiropodists from Wolverhampton. You know how fragile Doris is."

"Oh yes, terribly fragile...her wrestling career certainly got to her in the end," agreed Margaret. Katrina carried on. She was starting to enjoy herself again, and sat back to do the wistful gazing thing again.

"It was a tragedy for Sebastian, of course. He loves children. He once asked me to carry his love child, but of course I have dedicated my life to teaching brain surgery to five-year-olds."

"How terribly sad and terribly romantic!" exclaimed Olivia.

Katrina couldn't help but agree. It did sound sad and romantic.

Olivia continued, "Our poor darling Sebastian. He must be suffering so. With only one leg and a humectal chrondroplasmia, trapped in a loveless marriage with half a Frenchwoman and his only child raised by foot-loving strangers from the West Midlands. Goodness, Katrina, you must be his only delight. I believe we have you to thank for keeping him in such good spirits that he is able to tutor us so well in the fine arts."

"Hear, hear, thank you, Katrina. Will you join us for dinner later after the classes?" asked Margaret.

And then Katrina couldn't help herself.

(Please note that the following is a classic case of overegging the Pudding of Deceit. Many people – experienced liars as well as novices — make this mistake. "Just one more lie," they think, " and my work is done. I can saunter off into the metaphorical sunset, a sparkling trail of admiration in my wake. No consequences, no comebacks." But of course there are consequences and comebacks and jolly uncomfortable they are, too.)

"I would love to, but there's something else; I almost can't tell you, but it will be such a relief," said Katrina.

"Oh, do tell us, dear, you can count on us," said Olivia.

Katrina sighed her deepest and most convincing sigh. "Well, I need time to grieve. His illness is worse than you think. It's that humectal chrondroplasmia – the one is his vibula. It's spreading. Once it reaches his frontal anstruther, he will die. The specialists say he only has a month left to live. I almost can't bear it. Every moment is precious. I can't wait to see him again."

It was a lie too far... (told you).

Margaret and Olivia looked shocked and — Katrina noted uneasily and not without a twinge of guilt — saddened.

"Heavens! That's so dreadful!" said Margaret. Then suddenly she jerked her head up and looked past Katrina. Her reptilian claw clutched Katrina's arm even more tightly.

"But, darling, you won't have to wait very long to see him, for he's just got his black pudding and he's looking for somewhere to sit. He must be exhausted. Sebastian, over here!"

Katrina looked round to see a tall, handsome man approaching them. He was carrying his breakfast tray with aplomb as he strode towards them with just a hint of a limp.

"Oh no!" said Katrina, out loud rather than in her head, as she had attempted. "All this emotion is making me terribly dizzy. I simply must go and have a lie down. Bye, then!" She shook off Margaret's claw and scooted off in what she thought was the direction of outside. But it wasn't. She found herself trapped between the coffee machine and the cereals.

Sebastian watched her go, a curious expression on his face as he said, "Hello ladies, how are we today? Ouch!"

Margaret was out of her seat and had grabbed hold of Sebastian. "Darling, do let me take your breakfast tray. We're so sorry this will be your last week at the summer school. We'll miss you terribly!"

"But I have a five year contract!" said Sebastian, a puzzled look in his brown eyes (which were rather wonderful).

Margaret and Olivia, in their turn, looked puzzled.

"But surely the summer school people wouldn't engage you for five years in your condition?" said Olivia.

"My what?"

Olivia burst into tears. "Your squandula!"

"My what?"

"Your humectal chrondroplasmia!"

"My what?"

"Oh Sebastian, please don't die!"

"I have no intention of doing so. What on earth is going on?"

"But you're going to die! Your lover Katrina told us!"

"My lover? How dare you!"

"Don't be angry with us. It's Katrina. She told us all about it. We won't tell, we promise."

"Well, it's absolute rubbish! I'm utterly honourable. Since I married Doris I've never even looked at another woman, despite all our difficulties! It's ridiculous."

Olivia and Margaret looked at each other and then slowly understanding dawned.

"Margaret, we've been had. That Katrina is nothing but a little nobody trying to make herself somebody," Olivia snarled.

"I bet Sebastian's child hasn't been adopted by chiropodists! I bet he's been adopted by something dreadful like a coven of dramatherapists!"

"Ugh, yes. And I bet it's Katrina who hates the French!"

"And I suppose she's not a brain surgeon infant teacher, she's only a brain surgeon. And Katrina isn't even a real name!"

Sebastian was looking from one to another, trying hard to understand, his black pudding lying forlorn and forgotten. "Who is this Katrina? Where is this Katrina?" he asked.

"Where is she, Olivia? Look, there she is. She's trapped herself by the cereals."

Katrina saw they were pointing at her and her heart dropped to her knees, metaphorically.

"Oh no," she thought. "Where's my time machine? Please God, let it be half an hour ago and I'll never lie again. I might as well have stayed a boring, quiet mouse. It's better than being a liar. Well, I deserve to face my music."

Slowly she walked back over to them and sat down. Any minute now, she would feel the worst she would feel in her life. She looked at Sebastian. His eyes were the deepest, most wonderful brown she had ever seen. He was staring at her, those scrummy eyes full of raging emotion.

"So you're Katrina," he said slowly.

"Yes." Katrina felt deflated, defeated and very, very stupid.

"You're so… you're so…" Sebastian just couldn't get the words out.

"Yes, tell her what a disgusting little liar she is!"

snorted Margaret.

"You're so…."

"Yes, tell her how she'll be the laughing stock of the whole summer school!" brayed Olivia.

Sebastian paused. And then he said, "Katrina. You're so beautiful. Marry me!"

"What?" screeched Margaret.

Katrina beamed.

"But what about your wife?" squeaked Olivia.

"Never mind about Yvette. I hate the French," he said.

2 HAPPY GHOSTS

This story is not about happy ghosts. I have not written that yet. This story is about the time a meteorite fell into my garden, burning a hole through the cranium of a Bakelite gnome and ruining my prize courgette, Molly. As the annual winner of the Scruntly Bottom Vegetable Society's Veteran's Prize for Overweening Vegetables, I felt that the universe's wilful destruction of my opportunity to continue the theme extremely distressing. I confessed this to my current wife, Mrs Palfrey. "Mrs Palfrey," said I, as we both looked down at the disembowelled vegetable, "this distresses me."

"Why don't you call me Jean?" said Mrs Palfrey. "We have been married for over twenty years."

I feigned a feigned indifference to her comment, as I had done ever since we had plighted our respective troths before God and Man and the congregation of St Terpsichore all those years ago. If I had known that her father's do-it-yourself embalming business was to fail so dismally I feel I would never have married Mrs Palfrey at all. But she had, usually during a power cut, an intangible quality and a certain je ne sais quoi, too.

But if the truth must be told, and it must, otherwise

this story would not exist, I had grown tired of Mrs Palfrey. My feigned indifference hid a seething despair at the caprices of a life which had dealt out to me a weakening regard for Mrs Palfrey, a regard that diminished in inverse proportion to the attachment I felt for my vegetables, and in particular, for Molly.

Hence, my distress. Mrs Palfrey and I continued to look at Molly lying so nakedly exposed on the patio.

"Perhaps her death need not be in vain," I remarked, a germ of an idea breeding in my quick mind.

"Not at all. I am making ratatouille for dinner."

I pulsated with horror. How could Mrs Palfrey be so unfeeling, so callous? With difficulty, I pushed down the urge to cram my linen bandana into that cruel hole in her face, to stop her mouth forever. Instead, maintaining a self control as tight as Mrs Palfrey's father's wallet, I said, "I need some time alone with Molly."

When Mrs Palfrey had sighed a heavy sigh and clenched her fists until they were white, she walked stiffly back across the patio and into the kitchen. The evening silence was despoiled by the passive-aggressive clanging of matching oven-to-tableware.

But, at last, I was alone with Molly.

I picked her up gently, scraping at her delicate skin that had burned on to the patio. But as I lifted her, she fell to pieces. The sudden physical wrench tore my already metaphorically bleeding heart into a further metaphor, that of a triumvirate of pain, longing and grief. It was not just because the field was now clear for my rival, Lord Malcolm Bunton-Pargeter, to put forward Marion, his unfeasibly large marrow, for the Vegetable the Judge would Most Like to Declare Pope class and win. I have never yet won that class. Nor have I yet won The Grieves' Medal for Most Frightening Potato or The Rudest Carrot Ever. This latter class has been won for five years consecutively by Miss Prosser, the spinster organist at St Strictly's at Little Bedchamber, not two leagues hence away from here. But I digress. I was probably complaining about something. No, I remember I was expressing surprise of some sort. Ah, yes, the fact that Bunton-Pargeter, that plummy-mouthed fool of a trapeze artist, should at last gain the chance to lord it over me, twice literally as well as again metaphorically, did not stick in my craw as much as I had, at one time, feared it might. Had I known that the possibility of a Bunton-Pargeter victory would not devastate me particularly, I would never have desecrated his crops with a pea shooter loaded with pink food dye, night after summer night. Brilliantly, I'd ruined all his potentially champion vegetables except Marion the marrow, who remained tantalisingly out of reach, even when I gained a precarious purchase on the revolving compost bin and leaned dangerously over the fence that separated the Bunton-Pargeter territory from mine own. No, what grieved me most was the loss of my beloved Molly and her beauty: her creamy flesh now pulped, her delicate green skin shredded, burnt and torn, her soft underbelly revealed for all to see.

Although she was not, and never had been, an army courgette, I knew she must be buried with full military honours. It was what she would have wanted. The compost bin was just not fitting. I felt that her graceful sinews could only be paid full respect with nothing less than a blazing Viking burial at sea. But here at Number 43 Claudette Colbert Avenue, I lived a great distance from the pounding waves of the Channel which had so dutifully kept vast hordes of foreigners from blighting our royal shores for all these years, and, with not even a limpid lake or burbling brook within a short journey of the Ford Fiesta, I looked toward my pond, dimming languidly in the twilight of this forsaken day.

Expecting to see the balmy haze of soft dusk descending on this place of liquid sadness, a scene unblemished by surprising items, I found it instead blemished by surprising items. Or, at least, one surprising item. For there, at the edge of the pond, I saw the silhouette of a monstrous creature, beclawed and stripy, its snout guzzling the sweet pond water, a clutch of my prize Nymphaeaceae and no doubt some of my tiddlers to boot. One may within a traditional English garden expect a visit from, at best, an inquisitive badger or, at worst, an inebriated priest, but this took all manner of biscuits.

I realised at once that Morris the bandicoot had got out again.

I choked down the cry that leapt to my lips, as Morris was of the type Perameles Horribilis, which, you will understand, is the worst type of bandicoot — as big as a ping pong table, aggressive, mean-spirited and highly educated. Had I attracted his attention with my cry of alarm, he would no doubt have leapt to my throat and torn out my carotid artery not just with bestial enjoyment but with, no doubt, a philosophically detached air. And who would want to die that way? Certainly, not I. Instead, I dropped and rolled — those short but tragic weeks in the Scruntly Bottom Venture Scouts never having gone to waste — and hid behind a sharp-leaved yucca.

As I crouched, I pondered on Malcolm Bunton-Pargeter's choice of pets and cursed him freshly. Why my bespangled neighbour couldn't have a King Charles Cavalier like many of my annoying neighbours in Claudette Colbert Avenue was beyond me, but legend had it that Morris had saved him from a burning Big Top and in return Bunton-Pargeter had given him a good home ever since. I realised that the rogue meteorite that had destroyed my beloved Molly must have blazed through the lock on the Bunton-Pargeter conservatory, thus allowing Morris to escape.

"Molly!" I thought. In my haste to gain cover from possible Morris attacks, I had clean forgotten Molly, and judging by the whitish green smears about me, I had, to escape exsanguination by bandicoot, managed to spread her even further round the garden.

If you could understand the guilt and remorse that my

spirit outpoured at the shock of my own thoughtlessness, you would not only be an extremely empathetic reader but possibly one whose life has been besmirched with similar tragedies. As a fellow victim of Fate's whimsies, I salute you. But never mind that, because suddenly I heard a crunching sound and through the pointy yucca leaves I saw the glimmer of rising moonlight on glittery tights. At once I realised that Lord Malcolm Bunton-Pargeter, still the most exasperating of all titled trapeze artists, was in my garden.

"What ho!" came the familiar voice, hailing me from the other side of the yucca. "Don't worry, I've got Morris covered and I'll soon have him back. You can come out now."

I rose cautiously and was greeted by the sight of Bunton-Pargeter bedecked in his plain day clothes: pink satin blouson with aqua jacquard jerkin, the frills of which fell gracefully to his spangled tights and set off his neat shimmering Lurex-trimmed brogues. The steel glint of the 12-bore rifle he was holding reflected almost poetically his marquesite-studded braces.

"Sorry I'm a bit informal, I was just having supper and I never dress for dinner on a Thursday," he remarked, followed by, "Down, Morris, bad boy! Get back to your conservatory at once!" to, presumably, Morris, who had become bored of the pond and was rootling around behind the compost bin. Something there seemed to have interested him.

"Bunton-Pargeter," I said, feeling that I should take charge of the situation, it being my garden, "please remove yourself from my territory and take Morris with you. I really don't have time for this. Molly is dead, cleft in at least twain by the meteorite. Look at her! My girl, destroyed…."

Bunton-Pargeter cast his eyes round the garden and, to be fair, seemed dismayed at the courgette guts that littered the patio.

"Damn shame, Palfrey, old man; looks like neither of

us will win any prize this year. The dashed meteorite took out my beloved Marion too, and what with my other vegetables being pinkified, there's nothing I can enter this year. We'll both have to watch that toadying dankbucket Colin-Thomas Hornbeam of Chilleyhamptons take the prize. Perhaps I'll buy you a gin and we can jeer at the little rotter together."

I was overwhelmed. Bunton-Pargeter was suggesting we join forces to belittle Hornbeam in his moment of triumph. Was this outpouring of brotherly togetherness mere persiflage, or did it mean true friendship? Perhaps Bunton-Pargeter wasn't the fool I had taken him for, after all. Dazed by the emotional whiplash of the afternoon, I felt that team spirit was something I could do with.

"God damn it, Bunton-Pargeter, you're right," I said, feeling I needed to match his speaking style which had gone out with pince-nez and plus-fours. Feeling more confident, I edged forward and stood a hand clasp's distance from Bunton-Pargeter and his 12-bore. Morris failed to be interested in tearing my throat out, and continued to worry at something underneath the compost bin.

"I shall need help in burying Molly," I said, in what I thought was a hesitant yet commanding tone, offering Bunton-Pargeter the chance to set a seal on our friendship. "I thought nothing less than a Viking funeral?"

"Dash it, yes!" said Bunton-Pargeter, "I have half a melon skin that could serve as a boat and enough lighter fuel to burn down nos. 23 – 37 Claudette Colbert Avenue. That should do it. I only wish I could be as attentive to my garden tragedies. I've had to provide mass graves for my crops; there's too much carnage for individual honour."

He dropped his voice, and his whole body sagged.

"They're all dead, Palfrey. Even Marion. It's only Morris that makes my life worth living. You and Molly had it all, Palfrey. I've envied you for so long. It's so lonely on that trapeze."

I felt a new emotion. Empathy. I surprised even myself, but afore I could extend a pint of the milk of human kindness, he jerked his agonised face heavenwards and his voice rose and clanged like a wrong'd god atop Olympus.

"Why, if I ever catch that damnable rogue that ruined my crops!" he roared, shaking his Belgian lace-encrusted fist to the skies.

Unfortunately for me, Morris chose that moment to trot out from under the compost bin, carrying in his terrifying maw a pea shooter and a can of Kolour Me Bootiful food dye in Hot Pink. Bunton-Pargeter stared at the evidence that incriminated me so awkwardly, and then turned dangerously towards me, the 12-bore weaving out of control, his face a lashing of fury and betrayal.

"Wait, Bunton-Pargeter old chap," I said, hoping that my choice of tone and vocabulary would calm him, "I can explain."

Bunton-Pargeter now stood calmly, icily so. His instant mood swing terrified me more than the 12-bore, now pointed at my very vitals.

"Explain," he said.

Never had I thought so quickly, and so fruitlessly. Then suddenly, the answer came.

"It was Mrs Palfrey."

If I had hoped that shifting the blame to an innocent woman would get me off the hook, that hope was misplaced.

"Mrs Palfrey is a goddess. Besides, she is too short to climb on to that compost bin and too saintly to fire pink dye from a pea shooter on to my vegetables. You damnable liar."

I made the decision to back away, at first delicately, then in haste, as Bunton-Pargeter raised the gun. He hesitated.

"I ought to kill you here and now, Palfrey, but I won't. I abide by the Trapeze Artists' Code, which is to never kill a living being, even one as pathetic as you. I shall make a citizen's arrest." He started to lower the gun.

I saw my chance. I bolted. But Morris was faster, and several things happened very quickly that were my earthly undoing. It would be so much easier to inform you of the issues in a 7-point list format than try and explain it in a compelling narrative without getting all the "he's and his'" mixed up. You know what I mean; "He shouted out a warning, then he punched his face but before he could counter, his phone rang and it was his father-in-law asking if he had got the baker's order in as he was off to the funeral on Tuesday." That kind of thing. So a list of issues is what I am going to write and here it is below:

Issues of my earthly undoing:
1 I dodged backwards, but slipped on a bit of Molly and went reeling over.
2 Morris jumped towards me, knocking Bunton-Pargeter's gun arm.
3 The 12-bore fired.
4 The bullet took me through the heart, and I was dead even before I hit the herbaceous border.
5 My last human thought was, "Dash it to hell and back, how ironic."
6 Bunton-Pargeter remarked, "Gosh, sorry Palfrey, old man, that wasn't supposed to happen."
7 My first ghost thought was, "Well, this is jolly nice."

Point 7 above relates to the fact that suddenly I felt rather warm and lovely and was floating twelve feet above the scene of carnage below: mashed courgette, bandicoot droppings and a lifeless corpse. Actually, when is a corpse not lifeless? Discuss. But anyway, I know the picture below me sounds very much like a modern art installation but it didn't feel as threatening, as, being now a ghost and having a much wider view of things, I saw the whole silly business as my just desserts. I had been rather petty in life and unutterably mean to Mrs Palfrey and I felt somewhat troubled. I looked up at the universe and at the white light that is evidently always there but only the dead can see, and sighed a deep and manly sigh.

I looked down again and my heart warmed as I saw that Mrs Palfrey, disturbed by the sound of the gunshot, had come out of the house. She was holding hands with Bunton-Pargeter with one hand and patting Morris with the other. I knew then that all three creatures would be all right, and have long happy lives, and not be blamed for my demise, probably. I felt a tap on my shoulder. I turned and there was Molly, my spectral courgette, in one piece and beautiful again in her radiant ghosthood. I took her to my breast and we sailed upwards to heaven.

Oh look, this story is about happy ghosts, after all.

3 WHAT THE DOILY BIRDS SAW

The mountains in Kaiberistan in January are the coldest places on earth. Even if you were to sit in a big fridge with ice cubes stuffed down your bra, you couldn't be colder than Kaiberistan in January. Even if you were to sit in that fridge next to someone emotionally cold, like a Vulcan or Sherlock Holmes or your old maths teacher, and if they stuffed ice cubes down their bra too, well, you still couldn't be colder.

And because there was no firewood, no coal and no jelly to set fire to, the people of Kaiberistan kept warm by working hard. They worked at the spinach mines deep in the frozen valleys, lugging heaps of solid spinach up the winding mountain paths until the sweat ran from their brows and puddled in ice cubes in their turn-ups. They laboured day and night, chipping away at the rissole quarries, using pickaxe and shovel to force the frozen chunks into neat piles, ready for the goat carts to carry them away to the vegetarians of the Western Passes. They shouted loud and long, their breath steaming into their mobile phones, buying and selling diamonds, oat cakes, swans and wheat on the open markets and KFTSE 100 of the Kaiberistani stock exchange.

And the hardest worker, the man who worked longest, who lugged spinach furthest, who chipped rissoles quickest, and who sold swans and wheat loudest was Abdul bin Assallah, son of Abdul bin Assallah of the mighty Assallah clan of the mountain stronghold. Abdul Junior had a strong right arm, terse, muscular thighs and a voice that could shatter buckets at a thousand paces.

Abdul loved his work. After a long day's spinaching, risolling and swanning, when his tribe was asleep and shivering beneath the icy skies, Abdul kept on working long into the night. Working was his lifeblood and he had an ambition. An ambition that was the mother, father and stepfather of any other ambition in Kaiberistan.

His ambition was to turn snow into fire.

Each night, under the curious gaze of the moon, he experimented with snow and all the derivatives of snow he could find in the mountains: dendrites and columns, needles and graupels, granular firn, ice-lollies and slabs, pentitentes and even snirt, which is a real word. Every night for years he toiled, identifying just the right compound of snow, just the right crystalline structure, just the right centre of gravity until one cold January night, 17 years and four months after he first started his experimentation, it happened.

He knew he was on to something when he held a new compound of snow (SJ456_XP was its catalogue identifier) in his gloved right hand and added the secret ingredient — plain old snirt, but with eight (not six – fancy!) Bernie Quotients. (Bernie Quotients had been discovered accidentally by British scientist L J Bartley-Durward during a clay pizza shoot the previous May.) Slowly, slowly, the snow kindled in Abdul's hand. It kindled, it grew bright, it grew warm and then it grew hot; so hot and bright his clansmen woke to what they thought was the brightest and warmest sunshine that ever was.

And there was great rejoicing in the mountains. The snow fire grew, the normal snow melted and suddenly there was no need to work. People could keep warm just by being human. Some tribesmen took off their tank-tops to sun themselves on the rocks; tribeswomen took off their tights to paddle in warm mountain streams; and tribeschildren ran around naked, screeching for no reason, as all naked running children are wont to do.

"There's no need to work to keep warm any more. We can all relax and have a lovely time!" was the new mountain stronghold motto. This didn't go unheeded. The spinach mines closed. The rissole quarries shut. The Kaiberistani stock exchange locked its doors for the first time in 70 years since the Great Blancmange Disaster of 1911. And all the tribesmen chilled out and had fun, telling stories and making pancakes and playing rounders.

But Abdul bin Assallah wasn't happy. Now there was no work for him to do. He felt useless, restless, rootless. He didn't want to sit down with the rest of them and paint abstracts or play peep-behind-the-curtain or read the first half of important novels. He wanted to sweat, to work, to toil. He tried to interest the tribesmen in helping him build a new council estate, but they weren't having it.

"Why work, when you don't need to?" they asked.

So Abdul went off into self-imposed exile. He travelled the mountains in search of new work. But there was none. No goats to knit, no socks to fry, no tractors to explode. He felt useless, his virility compromised, his thighs thin and weak. In despair, he sat down by the side of a bright mountain lake, so still and beautiful that when he looked into it, to see if there were any fish to plaster, all he could see was his despairing reflection, a once proud, masculine tribesman with strong thighs now sunk to a dispirited workless fool.

So he cried. A big teardrop rolled down his cheek and fell into the lake, shattering his reflection into a thousand and three pieces.

"Hang on," he thought, "my reflection is broken. That will never do. I must make it whole again!"

So he dipped his hands in the clear waters of the lake,

to try to gather the pieces of the broken reflection into one whole person again. But the more he dipped his hands in, the more broken the reflection became.

Abdul was cheering up. He sensed a purpose.

"This reflection is still broken," he said. "I shall dedicate my life's work to making this right again."

So he dipped his hands into the rippling water again and again, ignoring the Butter Fish who came up to see what was going on, ignoring the Doily Birds, who circled above his head, puzzled about the man who gathered up empty water, moulding liquid into nothing.

He's still there now, 30 years later. He's working and he's happy. His tribesmen take it in turns get the bus over to sit with him and very often they bring him pancakes.

4 OLD MOTHER NASTY

Juniper Mildew was 118 years old and lived at Grunts' Cottage, the oldest house in Chipping Loveliness. When Juniper was a toddler and the guest of honour at her own christening party, her mother Mozzarella Mildew invited everyone in the village except for one person. This one person was Old Mother Nasty, the most evil woman in Chipping Loveliness.

The reason Mozzarella didn't invite Old Mother Nasty wasn't because she hated Old Mother Nasty or found her too nasty for a christening. The truth is that Mozzarella's brother Kettering had accidentally dropped Mozzarella on her head when she was little, and as a result she was a bit forgetful and ditzy. So she just clean forgot to invite Old Mother Nasty.

Now, in case you think this story is a bit like that fairy story Kipping Beauty or whatever her name is, and you expect Old Mother Nasty to storm into the party and set a curse on the whole blessed lot of them, you'd be wrong. Maybe you thought that when Old Mother Nasty saw the thread of happy guests making their way over the village green to Grunts' Cottage she fumed and spat and kicked Mambo her cat into the dishwasher. But you'd be wrong again. When Old Mother Nasty saw the procession of guests, she guessed that Mozzarella, in her silly, dizzy way, had forgotten her, but hadn't meant it horridly. So Old Mother Nasty sent over a lovely raspberry and nettle pavlova, a silver herring charm and a pretty card.

Before we get on to the atrocity that occurred on the day of little Juniper Mildew's christening, I need to tell you why Old Mother Nasty just sent a selection of nice things to the party rather than go over there herself. I also need to tell you why Old Mother Nasty isn't called Old Mother Nasty yet (we haven't got to that bit of the story), but I'll do that later. Just for now, all you need to know is that poor Old Mother Nasty suffered from agoraphobia, so even if she had been invited to the party she wouldn't have turned up. She was afraid to leave her house. So you would be forgiven, even by the most resentful of passive-aggressives, for thinking that this might be a bit of a non-story, what with the most evil woman in the village not upset at all about not being invited to a big party, and everyone else in the village enjoying a knees-up at Grunts'. But if you thought that, you would be wrong about that too. I know you're a busy person and you haven't got time for this sort of thing. I know you're tempted to move to the next story to see if anything is going to happen but hang on and we will get to the terrible incident shortly.

Despite you being wrong about two things so far, you are right to think that the polite and charming actions that Old Mother Nasty has heretofore displayed do not sound like the actions of the average evil woman. Indeed, Old Mother Nasty was the most evil woman in the village and yet so far has appeared to us to be rather pleasant. This is because evil is relative, and in Chipping Loveliness all the villagers were insufferably pleasant and notoriously good-natured, the kind of people you want to hate but can't, because that would make you scum. And you may have thought that in such an overwheeningly agreeable village like Chipping Loveliness, anyone who says

"Bugger!" when they drop a trug of dried neeps on their corns (as Old Mother Nasty did once in the corner shop, which had been the most evil act in Chipping Loveliness for centuries, and hence why Old Mother Nasty was the most evil woman in Chipping Loveliness) is likely to be labelled quite nasty. But you'd be wrong about that, too. You're not doing well today, but that is fine, I didn't do too well yesterday, what with the scimitar and the guide dog and court summons and all that, but that is a different story.

And although I am writing this in the relative safety of Notcutts (Cranleigh) Garden Centre's restaurant, sipping a latte which I got free with my Sage privilege card, I still feel a shiver of fear in my bones when I tell the story of what happened that day at little Juniper Mildew's christening party. Because Mozzarella Mildew was forgetful, and because Old Mother Nasty was agoraphobic, Old Mother Nasty was the first person in the entire village to witness the approach of the impending catastrophe. Is the word "impending" redundant here, if I've already said "approach?" I'm not sure. Please email me your views in nine words.

But can we go back to Old Mother Nasty's agoraphobia? I feel I have failed to explain it properly to you, and if I carry on with the story without explaining, you'll finish the story feeling a bit puzzled and I really don't want that to happen, not so early in the book.

The fact is that Old Mother Nasty's agoraphobia was due to a rare allergy to niceness. Niceness made her ill, and Chipping Loveliness was a pleasant village. You do the math. For those of you allergic to math (or "maths" for those that live here and not over there), here it is:

Allergy to niceness + Pleasant village = Unpleasant symptoms

Dr Tourniquet, the Belgian doctor who had settled in the village after his flight from Interpol, had diagnosed

Adult Onset Goodness Overreaction Syndrome. It meant
that pleasantries brought Old Mother Nasty out in a rash.
In the mornings she would begin her stroll to the village
shop with a calm epidermis but by the time she got to the
grocer's shop she had been the victim of a "Good
Morning! What a lovely day!" or "How are your corns?
Are you using that cream I got you?" which meant her
skin came up with lesions, and she was as scratchy as
pants made of Brillo pads by the time she got to the shop
doorway. If Colonel Harrumph opened the door for her
with his leering but sweet smile, she felt her throat close
up. If Sally Container behind the counter enquired
politely after her nephew in Llannerhys, she sneezed a
dozen times and put her back out. Old Mother Nasty felt
that if she witnessed one single act of selfless heroism, it
would finish her off. Even her own inherent niceness
gave her chronic allergic rhinitis.

So mostly she stayed indoors, too frightened to go out
because it made her so uncomfortable. She watched the
villagers go by. The villagers were sad because they liked
Old Mother Nasty. They liked her so much they called a
meeting in the village hall to decide how to help her.

The Mayor tickled his gavel (banging it would have
been too violent for Chipping Loveliness) and called the
meeting to order. First of all they sang Chipping
Loveliness' anthem *We are lovely and nice, all the time. We're
insufferable.* It goes like this:

(To the tune of *Onward Christian Soldiers*)

Verse 1
We are good and ni-i-i-i-ice
All the bloody time (*agitato*)
Villages around us (*crescendo*)
Think it is a crime (*subito piano*)
We don't think we're mental (*molto vigoroso*)
Or divorced from reality,
'Cos joy and hope are better for us (hold back the

time)
Psychologically

Chorus
We love buns and donkeys etc *ad nauseam*

After they had congratulated each other on the purity of their voices or clarity of their diction the Mayor asked them all to sit down with a cup of Old Betty and a custard cream and said,

"You all know why you're here. How can we help Miss Pretty-Buttercup? How can we stop her being ill all the time?" Miss Pretty-Buttercup was Old Mother Nasty's name prior to this meeting.

"It seems to me," muttered a shy young doctor at the back, "that if her illness is brought on by niceness, we're going to have to be horrid to her. That way she can't react so terribly."

"By the beard of Thor! That's ridiculous!" cried the Mayor. "We are nice, every man and lady jack of us! It'd be impossible."

"Listen to him, Mayor. What he says makes sense," said Dottie La Flange, the village's only petit-point tyre specialist. "Besides, he's an academic, so he must be right."

"Yes, but he doesn't know what he's talking about. He's not a doctor of medicine. He's a doctor of Cornish film studies."

"But he's all we've got what with Dr Tourniquet having to go into hiding again for a while, and, besides, I think I agree with him," persisted Dottie.

"Very well," said the Mayor. "We'll give it a go. We're going to have to teach all the children to be rude to her, or they will just muck it up. For a start we'll rename her Old Mother Nasty, even though she's not very old, she's never had a child and she has a very pleasant manner."

"Maybe we should call her Not Very Old Mother Nasty," said Gentle Colin, one of several village idiots.

"It's a bit nicer."

"No, we have to be nasty or we can't help her," they all said. "Gentle Colin, you are silly but we love you," they all continued.

And so it came to pass that the villagers started being mean to Old Mother Nasty, to try to help her. They found ways to help her that an independent witness might have felt to be inappropriate. Here are two sample scenes that an independent witness may have felt uncomfortable about witnessing, were they not in on it:

Grocer Jack (grocer) to Old Mother Nasty (OMN): Here's your veggie box, you old cow. Mind you eat the spinach quick, it's on the turn.

OMN: Thanks, Jack. I must say your aubergine last week was so succulent.

Grocer Jack: All part of the service, Fatty.

Or, on Tuesdays when Tom the paper boy came to collect the money for the week's papers:

Tom (paper boy): That'll be ten and six, wrinkly freak.

OMN: Here you go, Tom, and that's an extra bob for you. Thanks so much for stacking my coal so nicely yesterday.

Tom (still the paperboy): My pleasure. Why aren't you dead yet? Bye!

OMN: Bye, love. Tell your mother I said hello. (Cheery wave.)

And although the villagers were horrid to her, it didn't work very well, because she knew that they were only doing this to make her feel better. But they kept trying, and she kept appreciating it, which only made her allergic rhinitis even worse. So she stayed indoors and missed out on happy occasions, like Young Meriel's wedding to Jim Panty-Tiler of Panty Mansions, or the annual Dance of the Choughs each spring.

Anyway, all this has taken us a long way from Juniper Mildew's christening party, and Old Mother Nasty sitting

at her window watching the festivities around Grunts'
Cottage from her front room window.

She sat stirring her Old Betty, and enjoying the
atmosphere of the party as it presented itself to her from
across the green. She wiped her nose, which had started
to run because of the vibes of all the pleasantness and
shouts of joy from the little ones and the delight that Old
Mother Nasty took in that. She could see that in the
garden of Grunts' Cottage Billy Bob Mkebele was on his
grandfather's accordion — Billy Bob was half Inuit, half
Tring — and was leading Rotten Borough, the village
dance band. His uncle Black Hawk Pankhurst was calling
the dance. How Old Mother Nasty used to love the
Wiggle Bottom Rhumba, the *Hairy Mary* and the *Rampant
Skedaddle*. She started tapping her feet; her corns, scuffing
against the scorched-sycamore laughing-post of her
Tudor-inspired cubby, weren't bothering her at all today.
Rotten Borough had just finished playing the *Pleurisy Pogo*,
a great favourite with the old 'uns, and there had been
only minor injuries this time. Soon it would go on to
other old favourites: *The Stinky Weasel, Damn Yo' For a
Fool, Boy*, and her personal favourite *Eat My Begonias, Mrs
Dalrymple*.

But, 'ere she could hum along to the strains of *Wen
Maydens Do But Ope Theire Legges* — do remember to insert
a different song title if you are reading this to children —
out of nowhere, her nose dried up and she felt the first
dark wave of despair tug at the core of her very being. It
was as if a metaphorical blanket of the saddest-tasting
grief and misery-embracing dankness had entwined itself
about her soul, which she felt struggling to keep its little
soul-head above the sea of desolation it found itself in.

"Now, what is this all about?" mused Old Mother
Nasty, who had never been prone to needless bouts of
misery, feeling that life was too short for such emotional
extravagance. She looked round for Mambo the cat.
Instead of lying curled up in a happy-cat state of bliss in
front of her knitting, he was in a terrified-cat pose with

arched back and wide frightened eyes, on the top shelf of the bookcase, among the Jeffrey Archers that someone had given her as a joke, and she was too curious to part with.

"Existential angst is not my preferred option," thought Old Mother Nasty, "and Mambo is upset. So this bleak depression and terror we are both feeling must be coming from outside."

So Old Mother Nasty opened her front room window and stuck her head out, to get a better view of the village green. She saw the festivities at Grunts' Cottage, but turning her head toward the cricket pitch end of the green, she spied something that almost stopped her heart beating but at the same time made her eyes less itchy.

From the Batchester End of the pitch there spread a dank, dark, gloomy miasma — I checked the dictionary and it was definitely a miasma rather than a plain haze — a fog frightening and silent in its deliberate eerie quietness. Already it had blotted out the cricket pavilion and parts of the scoreboard so she could see only that the previous Saturday the Visitors had scored 164 for something with No. 6 not out on something else, most probably less than 164.

As the feeling of tragic hopelessness threatened to envelope her, she noticed that the cloud of doom actually had legs.

"This is surprising," she thought, a rampant curiosity overtaking an almost natural urge to make another pot of Old Betty and consider the situation. She watched further as out of the gloom, she saw emerge one, two, three — goodness, four! — men on horseback.

These were no ordinary men, and these were no ordinary horses. Old Mother Nasty could see this immediately. For a start, small banks of evil cloud and flies played around the men's heads, with flashes of mini-lightning lighting up their sharp features.

"Well, that's dangerous," Old Mother Nasty thought. "What a fire hazard, given that we've had a very dry

June."

Secondly, the men were rather tall and imposing, and their horses even more so. What was interesting about the horses was their curious colour and attributes, and what was strange about the men was their essence of pure evil. To help you visualise, I've compiled a list of their essential characteristics in note form as I am getting tired now:

Horseman A: Wore a crown and carried a bow. Essence: a macabre, creepy evil. Imagine Christopher Walken in Sleepy Hollow, but with a head. Horseman A's horse was white, shiny and breathing fire. Obviously feisty. Would have kicked the gumbo out of Lassie and not feel an iota of guilt.

Horseman B: Really, really cross. Wore a very big sword which probably had some Freudian meaning. Essence: an unpredictable, violent evil, like how that actor played Al Capone in The Untouchables, which I haven't seen for ages but enjoyed a lot despite Sean Connery taking an unfeasibly long time to die. Horseman B's horse was blazing red, looked hot to the touch and so a huge health and safety issue. Breathing fire, so similar to a dragon and Horse A but not either. Would have roasted Bambi with a single hiccup.

Horseman C: Carried a big pair of scales and a bit scary. That's pretty much all, really. Horse C was black with a highly polished surface. You could have done your make up in its side if you didn't mind being cleft asunder by its sharp and angry hooves.

Horseman D: Very, very skinny. Almost skeletal. Actually skeletal, really. Wore a hoodie. Horse D was green, not like the green of mushy peas but more like, let me see, Willow Tree by Dulux. Exactly that. Most unusual for a horse but not for a bedroom wall.

"Well, bless my soleus," thought Old Mother Nasty. "It's the Four Horsemen of the Apocalypse."

And indeed it was.

If you have never read Revelation or other novels or aren't St John the Evangelist, you may not have heard of these baddies. The Four Horsemen of the Apocalypse aren't pleasant at all. You don't want to get in the way of them, as they are known for being mean and spreading bad things like war, famine, disease and the other thing that I've forgotten for the moment but I'll come back to after a quick look at Wikipedia.

What was even more interesting about the men and horses, as if the above wasn't freaky enough, is that they weren't trotting in a straight line, like in films where horsemen come triumphantly out of the mist toward the camera. As Old Mother Nasty watched she saw that they were trotting forward, then stopping, then trotting backwards, then galloping forwards and across, all the time waving sticks and shouting at each other. And something was rolling between them, bumping and bouncing across the green. She heard fearsome shouts of,

"To me, to me…No! Wrong way! "

"Pestilence, you idiot, you've crossed the line of the ball improperly! And we were up!"

"That was some unsafe hooking there, Death! Do you want to kill me?"

The Four Horsemen of the Apocalypse were playing polo.

Old Mother Nasty didn't like the sight of this. Apart from the damage they were causing to the cricket pitch, and God knows there wasn't much left in the pitch repair kitty since the first eleven's night out at the All You Can Stuff Down Your Face Buffet and Grill at Batchester, she saw that the horsemen were gradually making their way across the green towards the party. And she knew by the swathes of misery she was feeling that the village was in danger. She looked toward Grunts'; the music had stopped. Rotten Borough had sat down, and thrown its accordions, ukuleles and dulcimers aside, as if music no longer meant anything. Some of the guests were gazing across the green, dazed; some of the guests had their heads bowed, as if they knew that all the joy of life was no longer theirs. Colonel Harrumph sat on the stone garden wall of Grunts' Cottage, playing with Chekov, his trusty service revolver, in the way that people who are considering a speedy exit from this world do. A solitary child, Daphne-Rose Engels, held on to the garden gate and whimpered. Mozzarella had come out of Grunts', a party hat limp on her mad hair, little Juniper asleep and grumbling in her arms.

Old Mother Nasty suddenly felt a bit cross. How dare these four horsemen ruin little Juniper's party? She opened her lead-lighted window and climbed out. She walked down her path, through the gate, over the road and onto the green. She stood with her hands on her hips at the side of the pitch and observed the horsemen more closely. She was a bit scared because they looked very fierce and any one of the horses could probably kill her in a variety of imaginative ways, but as her itchy skin had cleared up, and she could breathe much better, she carried on. She called out, "Excuse me, Horsemen. Don't you know you shouldn't be riding on the pitch? It'll ruin the bounce. Please dismount and lead your horses off."

As one evil entity, all four horsemen turned to her, and she could read the expressions on their faces … hatred, outrage, curiosity, more hatred. The thing they were hitting around came rolling and bouncing towards her, and stopped in front of her, looking up at her blankly. It wasn't a normal polo ball. With a shock, Old Mother Nasty recognised the dyed golden head of Candy Stanton, the postmistress from Chipping Glorious, the next village down the Batchester road.

That did it. This just wasn't cricket. Horrified, she stepped delicately over Candy's head and strode manfully out.

"Just what on earth do you think you are doing? Candy was due to retire in September. She'd already booked a caravan in Bognor. You've killed her and now she won't be able to go."

The four drew up to her, and stood very tall and looming. The scary horses were champing not poetically at a forest floor but at their bits of evil, desperate to take a bite out of Old Mother Nasty.

The one on the black horse spoke in loud, ringing tones, "Bow down before us. We are Pestilence, War, Famine and Death!"

"No!" hissed the one on the white horse, "I'm not Pestilence. I'm Conquest. Conquest!"

"You can't be Conquest," said the one on the fiery red charger. "I'm War and conquest is a bit like war, so you have to be something else and we all agreed you should be Pestilence. You're better at disease than fighting, anyway."

"Oh shut up, Steve," said the white-horsed horseman. "We've been through this. You're War, yes, but you're civil war; that's different from conquest."

"I don't care who's who," said Old Mother Nasty, feeling a strength that she hadn't felt for years. "Why are you here? You really aren't welcome, not today. It's little Juniper's christening party."

"A christening party? Fantastic! We've brought a present for the ickle baby," sneered the skinny one on the pale green horse. "But first maybe a plague of boils and death of the firstborn?"

The other horsemen chuckled in an evil way, reining in their horses, who were getting a little restive as they hadn't blasted, mown down or kicked anyone to infinity for a couple of days at least. But Old Mother Nasty was having none of it.

"Well, if you have a present, leave it here and be on your way."

"Oh," said the skinny rider, "we actually haven't got a present. Sorry, I love a party and just got carried away a bit. It's a shame we have to kill everybody, really. "

The one on the red horse looked like he was losing patience, and whispered, "Paul, shut it!" and then, to Old

Mother Nasty, "Woman, soon to die, we heard there's a tasty baby around here and it's our job to eat it."

"Then why are you wasting time playing polo instead of getting on with your work?" asked Old Mother Nasty.

"It's our day off," said the skinny one.

Old Mother Nasty looked more closely at the skinny one.

"Why, I can see your bones!" she said, then immediately felt embarrassed as she wasn't one to make loud personal comments. A wave of pity rose in her naturally kind breast. "Aren't you hungry? Wouldn't you like some food? We've plenty."

The skinny one hesitated.

"Well, actually, that would be ni…,"he began, but he was cut off by a roar of anger from War.

"Of course he's hungry, he represents bloody famine!"

"No, I don't represent famine, that's Famine," said Death, patiently. "I represent death," Death continued, "haven't you got that yet? I admit it's a bit weird that I, a skeleton, not representing famine, am skinnier than Famine, who does represent famine, but I think that's down to the philosophical and historical …."

"Shut up!" interrupted War rudely. "Woman, we don't eat stupid things like christening cake or pineapple and cheese on sticks. We only eat babies and other things that would cause sadness to others on devouring said babies and other things. And we don't bother about knives and forks with babies. It's not like fish, where you need a proper knife. We rip babies apart. Slowly."

"But that must make an absolute mess of your garments. Your dry cleaning bills must be huge," mused Old Mother Nasty.

"She's right," said Pestilence, "blood and brain matter are a devil to get out. I've always wondered why we have to do it that way. Sometimes I'd just prefer a sandwich on a plate."

"Shut up! Shut up!" screeched War. "Can't you see

what she's up to? She's being insufferably nice. Well, it will just make me want to pull her kidneys out though her mouth, rather than just behead her like normal."

"There's cheesecake," said Old Mother Nasty.

There was a pause.

"What kind?" asked Famine.

"Strawberry. And there's also a nice apple pie made by our own Dottie La Flange, and I think there are some Pringles left." She turned round to the guests waiting patiently but at the same time quaking with fear by the garden wall. "Are there any Pringles left?" she called.

"Yes," called back Mozzarella Mildew, "but we've run out of Sour Cream and Onion. Got Frazzles, though."

There was another pause.

"I like Pringles," said Pestilence.

Encouraged, Mozzarella Mildew dandled the sleeping Juniper a bit more, and called,

"We've got a selection of lovely real ales, too. Made by the microbrewery at Chipping Joyful, the other side of Batchester. There's Verger's Revenge, My Old Sock and I think we've got some Thunderguts in."

"Ooh, that's a good brew," said Famine. "I've heard it's really smooth with a honey-like timbre. But I've never tasted it. The twice I've been in a pub people just ran away screaming. Sometimes it makes me feel quite miserable."

"Shut up," whined War, but everyone felt that he didn't mean it as much as he did the last time he said it.

Death said, "I haven't had a pint of Thunderguts for years. Perhaps we could just have a half and a handful of Pringles and then only kill the women? Or maybe just the band? Maybe if we left the band's heads in a row on the pitch that would be enough?"

"Well, I think that would be impolite," said Old Mother Nasty, shaking her head. "You can't just gate crash a party, eat all the Pringles and then behead the band. It's bad form. We've had some lovely music today." She paused and then said, "Do you play anything yourself?"

Death grinned a happy grin, even more grinny than when he had a neutral expression. After all, his cranium was a head with the person scraped off so he couldn't do much else but grin, but he still managed to look happier when he spoke about music. "Well, I used to play guitar, but I just don't have time to practise now," he said. "I was quite good and I love Bob Dylan. You play, too, don't you, Steve?"

Steve/War said, "Oh, not for ages. And I play piano, too. Grade 4. But of course like you say, there's no time now, what with all the warmongering and being evil. I miss it." He looked wistful for a moment but then he shook himself and said, "But that's not the point. We have jobs to do. This is ridiculous."

Billy Bob Mkebele, Rotten Borough's leader, approached Death cautiously, holding out a slice of Battenberg.

"Would you like some cake, Mr Death? As a village we prefer Mr Kipling's Lemon Slices but there's always a place for Battenberg."

Death looked at the pink and yellow deliciousness and his little skeletal eyes gleamed. He reached for the cake with a bony hand and before anyone could say, "Crikey, I've never seen a skeletal figure eat cake as quickly as that!" he had wolfed it down. Even Blind Tony who you haven't met yet and who couldn't see very well, hence his name, could make out the pink and yellow chunks bouncing down through the bones of Death's ribs, and disappearing.

Death smiled even more and said, "That feels better! Thank you so much. I wonder, would you have any spare cake for my horse? I think he would like something other than the infant bones he usually gets. I think there's probably too much calcium in his diet anyway."

Old Mother Nasty agreed. "Everything in moderation," she said, but she was puzzled. Her eyes had started to itch again. Could this mean that evil was starting to recede and things were getting nicer?

Daphne-Rose Engels edged forward with a plateful of pink-iced fairy cakes with those little wormy sprinkles on top which one always feels one shouldn't eat but one does anyway.

"Can I feed your horse, Mister?" she said to Death.

"Of course," said Death, "but mind his hooves, they're very sharp."

"Why is he green? It's not normal for a horse, is it?"

Death and Daphne-Rose carried on their conversation as Daphne-Rose fed fairy cakes to Death's green horse, who enjoyed every mouthful so much that he forgot to trample the little girl to death.

"How delightful!" breathed Pestilence, who usually felt mopey and ill, but was looking on benevolently. "Such a pretty girl with a plate of fairy cakes. Look how her freckles echo the sprinkles on the cakes. I can really see a nice shot there," he said, photography being his hobby when he wasn't laying waste to entire nations through pandemics of one flavour or another. He dismounted from his steed, and gave the reins of his fiery white charger to Colonel Harrumph, who, despite his fear and despair, had in the last five minutes not been able to take his eyes off such a fine beast. He placed Chekov his still trusty service revolver down on the garden wall and stroked Pestilence's horse's nose.

"Lovely line and length," said Colonel Harrumph. "Good long stride, I noticed. Eyes bright, ears forward," he said. "The fact he breathes fire is interesting but I don't think they'll disqualify him for that if we entered him for the Chipping Loveliness gymkhana in September. What's his name?"

Pestilence felt a surge of pride run through his befurred arteries. "His posh name is something very long in Hebrew that I can't pronounce very well, so I just call him Monkey."

"Hullo, Monkey," said Colonel Harrumph, scratching Monkey behind the ears. Monkey breathed just the littlest of flames as if to say "I am a proud beast but nevertheless I am enjoying this scratching." Colonel Harrumph and Pestilence wandered off around the green, talking a perfect orgy of horse shop. Monkey ambled after them, snatching a tuft of grass here and a wicket there, tail swishing away Pestilence's flies.

Old Mother Nasty hadn't taken her eyes, which were still a little itchy, off the scene. She glanced at War, who was sitting on his blazing red charger, looking like a mythical baddy that was fast losing control of the situation and didn't quite know what to do about it.

She suddenly thought, "Oh no, where is Famine? Is he wreaking wretched havoc on the guests?" She turned round to face the cottage and was charmed to see through the window Famine sitting at the kitchen table, eating Pringles with a pint of Thunderguts and watching Dottie La Flange demonstrate the exotic art of fruit scones.

She turned back to War.

"It's just you and me now, War," she said, and she stepped forward a pace, then another. War turned to her squarely, his steed champing, restless.

"I see what you've done. You won't get away with it," he said and uttered a bellowing roar that echoed around the village and terrified the crows who rose from the trees in a crescendo of flapping and of alarmed crow noises. Everyone stopped, except Death and Daphne-Rose who were chatting about games Death used to play when he was little. But Colonel Harrumph and Pestilence turned around from the edge of the green, where they had wandered contentedly.

"Look, War," said Old Mother Nasty a little desperately, "it really doesn't have to be like this. Don't you get bored of beheading people and making people unhappy?"

"Well of course I do. It's dull, dull, dull taking people's heads off, day in, day out! But it's what I'm trained for and it's my destiny. You have to fulfil your destiny. Most of the time I'd rather embroider some cushion covers and have a little house of my own, with a little stream in the garden and newts, and maybe a Mrs War creosoting the fence while I flute the edge of a blackberry pie. Isn't that everybody's dream? But we can't, this is what we are born for. Death, destruction, plague and all that kind of stuff. So do me a favour, woman, and stand aside while I get on with the job of eating that little toddler and then killing everyone else. It's a bore and it does make me sad, but that's my job and I do have a sense of duty."

"If you had a sense of duty you'd help out with the washing up. And who says it's your destiny? Who told you to do all this killing and make people feel scared?"

War hesitated. "Well, I'm not really sure. We've just always done it. One day I woke up with a scary horse and lightning playing round my strong features, and there were these three mates on imposing horses and because everyone ran away screaming we thought we were horrible. We look evil and so do our horses and no one likes us. After a while you get fed up with feeling rejected. We're just horrible; that's what people expect so that's what we are. It's a vicious circle."

"We don't think you're horrible," said Mozzarella.

"You don't?"

"Not at all. Well, except for what you did to Candy."

"I'm not proud of that. None of us are, but we have to pretend to enjoy it. We can't stop now."

"Why not?" asked Old Mother Nasty.

"Because we've done it for years. If we stop now and become nice, that would literally be eons of badness committed for absolutely no reason. It would make our existence futile and furthermore if we change our minds now we would just look stupid."

Old Mother Nasty nodded her head sagely and pursed her lips. "I can see your issue. It's very similar to the crisis of faith suffered by Sally Container at the shop. For years she believed the Carolingian doctrine and abided by its tenets – you know, hopping on Tuesday only, no scones on a Friday, blessing the holy tractor and a week at Skegness each year mortifying her flesh and playing Bingo. But last year it just felt wrong. Didn't it, Sal?"

"Certainly," said Sally Container, who had heard her name and came out from under the ash coppice by the pond where she had been cowering. "I suddenly realised that if I believed I was right, then everyone else with a different belief must be wrong and really, if you think about it, that can't be right. And then I worried that because I had spent so many years believing things and acting accordingly and yes, slightly battily, I would have wasted all those years. And of course I thought that I would feel a bit silly if I changed my mind. But then I thought a bit more and decided that it's better to change my mind sooner rather than later. I've still got the rest of my life ahead of me, which of course might be pretty short if we can't convince you to change your mind, Mr War."

"Call me Steve," said War.

"And," continued Sally, "no one has laughed at me or said I was inconsistent. And I would have punched them in the fanny if they had, because I've taken up Tai Kwon Do and it's much more fun than tractor blessing."

"No one has made fun of you?" asked War.

"Not a soul," said Sally Container.

"But people scream and run away when they see us. We're never going to get a positive reaction."

"Look, Steve," said Old Mother Nasty, thinking she had one last shot, "try it for half an hour. Try being yourself, not your warmongering, scary self. Be Steve. Come in for a cuppa, tether your horse outside. Give it half an hour and if you don't think you can live a new way then, fine, eat the baby and kill us all."

"That's a bold strategy," thought Mozzarella, and hugged Juniper even more tightly.

"I've had enough of this!" roared War/Steve, whose anger, to be fair, had been stirred by his own self-loathing and fear of change rather than anything that Old Mother Nasty had said. He jumped down from his horse with another bellow that shook the very clouds and made them fluttery and nervous, so much so that some of them (mostly the cirrostratus, the cowards of the cloud world) fled away to the next county to watch from there. War strode over and grabbed the revolver that Colonel Harrumph had left on the garden wall. He jumped back on to his steed and pointed the gun at Old Mother Nasty's forehead. Everyone gasped and backed off.

Except Old Mother Nasty. She stood as still as Time when he/she/it stands still, and stared up at the shortish barrel of the gun, knowing that one false move would mean certain death for her and a fairly certain and most unpleasant death for everyone in the village. A wave of fear enveloped her all the way from her fast-clearing-up skin to her not-so-aching bones.

"Steve!" called Pestilence, from the other end of the green. "Put the gun down. Let's all be pleasant! I'm so enjoying it! Colonel Harrumph has told me some remarkable stories about his school days — he's an Old Corruptian, you know – and it sounds like such a wizard wheeze!" And Famine had run out of Grunts' Cottage, holding up a baking tray in a mannerism protective of Old Mother Nasty but not useful as such. Death hadn't noticed anything as he was too engrossed in playing cats' cradle with little Daphne-Rose Engels up on the cricket pavilion steps, so he missed all the action.

"No!" wailed War/Steve. "I can't change. It's too late!" The gun quivered in his hands. His finger tightened round the trigger. Everyone held their breath.

"Excuse me, War," said Old Mother Nasty quietly, with just a hint of a quiver in her pleasant alto voice. "I don't mean to interrupt you in your hour of angst, but why do you need a gun to kill me? Can't you just blast me with satanic lightning or any one of your panoply of evil powers?"

War thought for a moment. "I could do," he said,

"but perhaps the author of this story felt the need to add more drama to the closing stages. Some readers might think you're getting off too easily. No one finishes a story with a well-reasoned argument. There needs to be a gun and a tense stand-off situation, that's a given, and someone who is emotionally unbalanced and could go either way. That's me. We have to think of the American market." He paused, and then a big tear rolled down his face. "Don't you understand how hard it is to be evil all the time, but how it's even harder to change?"

He paused again, and then "Weakness!" he cried at himself, and clutched the gun a tad more firmly, as if to convince himself that he really was going to shoot. Everyone carried on holding their breath, some turning slightly blue in the process. Old Mother Nasty closed her eyes and waited. She felt very sad as she really liked her life and didn't want it to end just yet.

War let out a small sob and straightened his arm to fire. The click of the safety catch coming off was very loud in the quiet of that summer day. The click woke little Juniper up and the first thing she saw after her dreams of puppies and lollipops and Mummy hanging out washing in sunlit fields was War looming and aiming his gun at Old Mother Nasty. She saw his sharp features, the lightning playing about his head, his terrifying steed hissing steam and drooling green slime. Juniper opened her eyes wide, and then her mouth, and everybody waited for the inevitable wail, followed by War getting embarrassed, shooting Old Mother Nasty and then blasting them all to shreds.

But then, amazingly, little Juniper Mildew chuckled. She pointed a chubby finger at War's horse and gave a big baby grin, and drooled a little just like the horse, but not greenly.

"Horsey!" she burbled. "Nice man! Pretty lights!"

War turned sharply around.

"You mean me?" he said, the gun forgotten in his hand.

"Ess!" ("Yes") said Juniper. "Nice man! Horsey dribble!" and she let out a rollicking, brambling, sparkling chuckle that would melt the heart of every demon in hell should demons have hearts to melt. With her plump baby hand she held out to War half a digestive biscuit that had been gummed a bit so was soggy at the edges.

"Bickie!" she said. "Play!" she went on, pretty much exhausting her vocabulary.

Mozzarella set Juniper on the ground and the toddler started to do what toddlers do best. She toddled, mostly in the direction of War.

"She wants you to play with her," Mozzarella said.

"But I don't know how to play with babies," said War, "I only know how to eat them."

But after watching Juniper's broad toothless smile and bandy, wobbly legs, he brightened. He dismounted from his horse and placed the gun carefully back on the wall. He looked down at Juniper who had reached him and was steadying herself using his trouser leg as purchase. War took a deep breath in and said, "Hello, toddler. Would you like to see my collection of shrunken heads?"

"Ess!"(again,"Yes") said Juniper brightly.

"I'm not sure that's suitable for babies…," began Sally Container but Mozzarella interrupted. "Actually, I think I'd like to see them, too, Mr War. I did advanced anthropology with sociology at St Mungo's but I missed the shrunken head module when I was off eloping with Juniper's father, God rest his soul."

Soon War was in the middle of an interested bundle of villagers who all wanted to see his collection. He was holding Juniper tenderly under one huge arm while they passed round the heads. Juniper was trying to catch the lightning that played about War's own head, and giggled every time her finger buzzed with a strike. Someone handed War a glass of Pimm's with a straw and gave a doughnut to his horse, who had been chewing off the gate post of Grunts' Cottage.

Old Mother Nasty looked around. War was smiling

and enjoying the admiration of the crowd. Pestilence was bouncing alongside Colonel Harrumph, who had a very fine seat upon Monkey and was attempting some horse ballet with added flames. Famine had produced some scrumptious-looking scones after Dottie La Flange's tuition and was serving them with the finest Batchester clotted cream to Rotten Borough, which was hungry and weak after all that fear and misery. Death and Daphne-Rose were now playing hopscotch and some of the other children had skipped over to play with them.

Old Mother Nasty breathed a heavy sigh of relief. "It looks like everything is going to be alright again. But I do feel bloody awful," she thought. And she did. All the relief at not being killed or eaten plus all the fun the villagers were having with the now beautifully-natured horsemen made her feel very happy, so her old allergies to niceness struck her with full force. Hearing that Rotten Borough, who had wolfed down their scones and begged for more, had struck up *24 Hours From Ulster* and seeing that all the villagers and the horsemen were playing, chatting, cooking and generally having a nice time, she started to walk home across the green. Every movement was slow and painful. Her breathing was heavy and she really wished she had brought her inhaler with her. Her skin was itchy and all she wanted was a cool bath in lavender water. Her nose was running so hard but she had forgotten her tissues. Her throat felt like it was made of broken glass. She felt so horrid that she started to cry.

She was nearly at her garden gate when she heard a thundering behind her. She turned round and there was Pestilence, breathing heavily from his sprint.

"Where are you going? Don't you want to party? Famine's making one of Delia's," he said and then, "What's wrong?" as he saw her tears.

"I'd love to join in," Old Mother Nasty sniffed, "but I'm allergic to fun and joy and it makes me feel so ill. I've had this for years and I've tried to cope but I'm really fed up with it all now. I'm going to have to move somewhere

where the people are horrible, just so I can feel better. That will heal my body but it will destroy my soul." And Old Mother Nasty sobbed sobs that you would have found unbearably heart-rending, had you been there to witness this touching scene.

"Well, why didn't you say so?" said Pestilence. "Don't be sad. I'm not called Pestilence for nothing, even though that makes no sense. Yes, I can give out any disease you like, but I can also take it back again."

"You're a healer?" asked Old Mother Nasty, so taken aback that she burped slightly amid her tears.

"Well, I've never thought of it like that before," said Pestilence, "but I suppose I am. Here, give me your feet."

So Old Mother Nasty sat down on the pavement and took off her boots and socks. Pestilence, with deft and gentle hands (very surprising, given he had been a baddy for eons and used those very hands to dish out diseases like Mangot's Pudding and Haemohorridia as well as Scrofula, which I think is actually a real disease but shouldn't be because it sounds made up) examined Old Mother Nasty's feet.

"Oh dear, terrible corns. I'll sort those out, too." And so saying he rubbed the soles of her feet very firmly and muttered an incantation that only pre-dead Egyptian mummies would have been able to understand. Old Mother Nasty felt a warm, tingling sensation travel from her feet all the way up to her head, and suddenly she felt unitchy and clear-lunged, free-jointed and with the clarity of nostrils that only a very strong mint can give, but without the pain.

Old Mother Nasty whom, as we have previously seen, was not emotionally incontinent, felt so happy that she cried even more than when she felt horrid.

She stammered her thanks to Pestilence. "Pshaw!" he said. "Think nothing of it. Come on, would you like to dance?" He carried Old Mother Nasty back to the party and they whirled and staggered with the rest of the villagers to the strains of Rotten Borough's R and B cover of *Dang It, There Goes Another Button*.

I could tell you that they all lived happily ever after. But that would be a lie, as Candy Stanton stayed dead. Her head was buried, along with the shrunken heads, in the Hanging Gardens of Panty Mansions (a relic of the tourist-lynching days of yore), and she is still honoured each year in the Candy Stanton Film Festival, where villagers and ex-Apocalypse Horsemen show their favourite films on the green during warm summer nights.

But mostly, everyone did live happily ever after. The horsemen decided they liked it so much at Chipping Loveliness that they set up home there and integrated well. They were given the West Wing of Panty Mansions to live in, and their horses had the run of the meadows and enjoyed giving pony rides and carrying people's shopping for them every day. Pestilence assisted Dr Tourniquet, who had emerged from hiding, and no one was ever ill again, which gave Dr Tourniquet lots of free time to learn about bears. Sometimes Pestilence gave the countryside a plague of bees when the bees started running out, or a plague of butterflies and white doves especially for weddings. Famine enjoyed a reputation as an excellent cook and he and Dottie La Flange opened a very successful tea room, "Famine and Dottie's Famous Bun Emporium", a name that Famine felt was overdoing it but Dottie really liked so he just went with it. Death was a big hit with the kids, and he couldn't go anywhere without trailing at least half a dozen of them, who demanded to play Flight of the Bumble Bee on his ribs or repeatedly asked him which bone the knee bone was connected to, although it was pretty obvious.

As for War, what he liked best was to sit with Old Mother Nasty in her front garden on summer evenings, sharing a pot of Old Betty and a slice of Abigail's Tansy, with Mambo the cat purring on his lap. Together they watched little Juniper Mildew grow up into a fine, feisty and clever young lady who later made a name for herself through her famous quest for the world's fourth most mystical and edible oracle – the Cheese Pie of Secrets.

But that, of course, is another story.

5 HOW MAGNUS SOUTHEBY WAS BUILT

Dave had been a town planner all his life. He loved towns. He loved planning. So after he got his first class degree in Planning Interesting Towns, he landed his dream job — Assistant to Specky Cartwright, of Cartwright, Bell and Mahogany, the town planners' town planners.

Dave did well there. His inspiration was Specky and his magical pencil. After months of observing Specky at work, Dave learned all Specky's techniques but the imagination was all Dave's. With a flip and a gibbert of a 2HB pencil racing across crisp tracing paper, Dave brought into the real world a spaghetti of lucid, fluid roadways garnished with sturdy bungalows for the olds, chic flatlettes for the young and stalwart four-bedders for growing families. Not content with spacious and sunny squares, he added cheeky libraries, cheery post offices, soothing schools for the kids and cosy hospitals for the ill — all the things you'd want in an interesting town. Graceful gardens, majestic boulevards and cosmopolitan piazzas; everybody wanted to live in Dave's towns. Surely you've heard of Melchett Posterior, voted Town of the

Century? Haven't you admired the stone-cladded swans of the lido at Gravelly St Gerard? How about the neon flying buttresses of the Cathedral of St Kevin at Porton Bicuspid? That was Dave.

Dave's work was in all the shiny Sunday magazines and on those Sunday evening culture shows where bearded men and bald women use phrases like "ideological fecundity" or "tenacious thread of veracity." Artists thought he had an extra muse, just for him. Normal people thought he was smart and practical. Everyone loved Dave's work.

Except Dave.

"There's something missing," he thought, as he drew some Fibonacci shell spiral friezes into the concrete walls of a tar factory. "But what can it be?" he went on, as he added a palm tree plantation to a Tesco's loading bay. He carried on, musing and drawing and squinting in bad light. Dave's work was perfect. But, then, as he finished a swirl of mosaic pineapples for the moat bridge of a community health centre, he realised what the problem was.

He was bored.

But he carried on, creating places and spaces that oozed charm or quirk, pleasing everybody but himself.

After five years of staring into space and staring into the future, drawing details only he could see and going through pencil after pencil, Dave needed specs. Then he needed stronger specs. Then he needed even stronger specs, specs that were the size and shape of milk bottles. But he carried on working, carried on creating joyously inhabitable towns. And later, when Specky retired, he made Dave head of Cartwright, Bell and Mahogany.

One day, Dave received a letter from Whitehall. A secret man in the government had decided that Dave's towns were too nice and that his housing stock was getting too lovely for its foundations. The secret man decided that because Dave's towns were so popular, people in horrible towns were moving there too quickly and being too happy. The secret man thought happy people were a threat to the government, because they could focus on bigger things than how horrid their town was. The secret man wanted people to live in little house-like boxes with no room to store their ironing boards, and with ceilings so gloweringly low that tall men had to stoop just to sit on the toilet. The secret man in the government wrote a letter to Dave, which is the one he received at the beginning of this paragraph.

The letter said that the government wanted a new town planned and built; a big, bustling town that would outsmart all the other towns of the land. The government wanted the town in straight lines criss-crossing each other with a regimented vista of breeze block and wire. It wanted high densities in strange places, cars to take precedence over people, and playgrounds made of concrete and cat litter for the children to fall over in, because it was cheaper than that bouncy stuff around the statue up Lion and Lamb Walk in Farnham. The town was to be called Magnus Southeby.

Dave peered through his thick glasses at the government's letter. He knew at once that this new town was going to be another Silbury Keynote, that horror of a town where even three minutes there made people understand more about the futility of human existence. He pursed his lips and said "Hmm." And then he slowly crumpled up the letter and very carefully placed it in the bin.

Sitting at his big oak desk, staring at a blank piece of drawing paper, he was ready to create the new town of the millennium, Magnus Southeby. But not the one the government had ordered. This was to be the town of towns of towns, the work of his life.

Dave was no longer bored.

So, he started to plan and then he started to draw. And then he realised he couldn't see anything but blurry outlines, fading at the edges. But he carried on.

"I am a town planner," he said, "and I will plan this

town."

As he drew, he closed his eyes and he flew into his imagination, and working more and more quickly he powered through his fantasy of how towns should be, the lyrical pieces that make up a living space fit for the gods. And when he had finished, he opened his eyes and looked at what he had produced. And realised he couldn't see it. He couldn't see anything at all.

His assistant, Colin, came to pick up the design to take it to the town makers. Colin looked at the design and goggled. Then he goggled some more.

"Dave, are you sure about this?" Colin said, a bit sadly, because he had always liked Dave.

"I've never been surer," said Dave. He put his pencil down, stood up from his broad oak desk, felt for his coat and put it on. Feeling his way inch by inch to the door, he left Cartwright, Bell and Mahogany, never to return.

And if you've ever been to Magnus Southeby, you'll remember it. You will remember seeing the winding roads lined with diamanté and malachite, the pink bungalows built of jelly with the rooms on the outside, the skyscrapers deep underground and the parks planted with Californian Redwoods and aromatic chutney bushes. You can't have forgotten the Mosque of St Peter and the Cathedral of Mohammed, soldered together with one entrance and a place for velvet shoes, prayer mats and cassocks. You'll never forget the classy squares populated with wild boar and red squirrel, the libraries serving cake with mime at tea time every day (except early closing on Wednesdays when the librarians hit the knitting and ju-jitsu circles) and the all-weather poetry Jacuzzi, built of the finest marble and Anatolian lapis lazuli.

The secret man in the government was very, very cross.

6 AUNT GLADYS FAILS TO RETURN

A confusing story. I have to keep this in because it links with another story further on. Just go with it, it will be fine.

Chapter 1 (Don't worry, there aren't any more chapters.)

There was I, waiting at the church, thinking that there might be a song in my situation, when I realised I had been waiting at the church for over 18 years and that my Aunt Gladys was not likely to come back for me now. Aunt Gladys had dropped me at the church of our village Osgood Thoroughby when I was ten so that I could play on the gravestones while she picked up a couple of hoof pasties from the hoof pasty shop for a bit of lunch for us both. Aunt Gladys, with her embroidered hessian shopping bag, sensible low-heeled shoes and spider tattoo on her neck, had not shown up again. Besides, the hoof pasty shop had closed long ago, during the time of the Kanzai Uprising. The cairns by the roadside are still honoured today.

But back to the action, what little of it there is. My

Aunt Gladys had raised me lovingly since I arrived at her house by courier when I was a baby. I had been wrapped not in swaddling bands but in bubble wrap, with a hole for my head end and some kitchen roll for the other. Aunt Gladys signed for me and took me from the delivery man. She told me later that although she had initially been disappointed because I wasn't the new bread maker she had ordered from John Lewis, she had always wanted a baby and therefore she was very happy with me.

"And if I ever had a baby myself," she told me later while she defiantly ironed her armbands, "I'd rather have had it delivered by courier than by Caesarean or the usual method, which is a barbaric practice. If you can tell me how to get a pineapple through a ring doughnut without bursting it then I might just consider the usual method, but signing for a baby is so much easier and less likely to give one piles."

She was a very sensible lady, my Aunt Gladys. Or is, for it may be possible that she is, unlike my parents, still alive.

I can hear you thinking, perhaps aghast or perhaps casually, "What happened to your parents?"

I am not actually in your brain and nor do your thoughts speak aloud unless you are wired a bit like my friend Timothy-Jane; this is called a figure of speech, I believe. But I will tell you what happened to my parents, whether you are interested or not.

It is a sad tale, and if you are reading this you are more than likely a relative who has bought this book out of pity for me, so you already know the tragedy. But if you are not related to me, I can now tell you that my parents Colin and Jean Scarabond, of the Slough Scarabonds, were killed in a mysterious incident just after I was born.

I was born in Somerset, where my mother and father had holidayed during happier times. While my mother was pregnant with me, they journeyed to their holiday hovel at Sticky St Richard near the Dorset border to avoid the outbreak of Arabian Mumps that was devastating the poorer families of Osgood at that time. I was born in that holiday hovel, and I have a distant memory of staring grimly up at a mobile made of Fanta cans and dead beetles. Nevertheless, I feel sure that I was happy. Unfortunately, only one of the three of us returned from that holiday hovel alive. That was me. I don't know who found me alone in that hovel and had the brazen cheek to courier me to my Aunt Gladys, especially as I was, and still am, allergic to rubber bands and Lycra, but I suspect this unknown person may be the nub of the story. That's why my Aunt Gladys, on the run from the Rubbish Circus, ended up raising me.

Aunt Gladys was the main Osgood Thoroughby source of lemon drizzle cake and was always covered in a thin detritus of plain flour and icing sugar. She had been covered in detritus of one sort or another ever since she ran away from the Rubbish Circus to be with her sister, my mother Jean Scarabond. The Rubbish Circus was, as its name suggests, rubbish. It had acts like the Bearded Man and the Weeping Statue of St Christine-by-the-Skip, a weeping statue which didn't actually weep; instead it sniffed slightly and sometimes blew its nose. The good thing about being on the run from the Rubbish Circus, or any circus for that matter, is that you know where it is going to be on tour, so all you have to do is avoid that place while it is there. Aunt Gladys came to Osgood Thoroughby where the Rubbish Circus never came and where Jean Scarabond her sister had settled with her husband (my father) Colin, under a witness protection scheme after the Redolpho Affair. So Aunt Gladys was never caught by the Rubbish Circus, not even by their clowns who, disguised as other clowns, stalked the seaports to carry off unwary drunks to raise as protoclowns or bareback riders. Again rubbish, as there were no proper horses in the Rubbish Circus, just semi-naked men giving each other piggy backs. Or at least that's what they told the police they were doing.

So, back to me waiting at the church for my Aunt Gladys. Immediately upon realising that Aunt Gladys was never coming back, I resolved to find her. First I needed some new clothes, having outgrown the ones I was wearing when I stopped to wait by the church over 18 years before. While I had waited, many kind people of Osgood Thoroughby had given me clothes to wear but I had never really liked the cut or line of many of the donations. I feel sure that the Norfolk Jacket will never come back in to fashion, even in Norfolk.

Luckily, I had grown friendly with Father Mother, the vicar of the church at which I had waited. Father Isambard Mother had been vicar at St Linoleum's even before Aunt Gladys had ventured to the pasty shop. He liked me because during my 18 years' waiting for my Aunt Gladys I had helped him out with his duties. For example, when he had a heavy sermon on, he practised a particular hellfire move of slamming his scaly fist down on the lectern to dramatise the importance of goodness or to wake up the congregation. I marked him out of ten for sternity, fiery gazing and thundery magnitude, and he appreciated my high standards. Sometimes we shared a bottle of communion wine as I helped him stack the pennies from the retiring whip-round. Father Mother often gave me his cast-off vestments of which he had grown weary, so that most of the time I was mistaken for a youth of the cloth, and often hailed as "brother" or "father" when the truth is I was, and am not, either of them.

I started my search for Aunt Gladys on the Feast of St Taggart, patron saint of lost aunts and misplaced car keys. With a stash of communion bread and a slice of cold pizza in my man bag, I threw on my gabardine Geneva gown and preaching bands, placed my bejewelled zucchetto (stolen, I later discovered, by the Free Nuns of Port Sunlight from the sitting pope, Pope Ulvaeus) upon my head, picked up the gauntlet (kindly donated by our own Osgood Italian mediaevalist Kenneth Brouhaha, to keep my remaining hand warm) and set off to the where the pasty shop used to be, to find out what had become of my Aunt Gladys.

Not to be continued.

7 BUTTERFLY AND THE ICE AGE

Butterfly, a very pretty Golden Fairywing of London, stretched her shiny wings, ready for the new afternoon ahead. She'd been napping, perched on an aromatic frond of one of the palm trees of the Westminster Palm Forest that had sprung up during the Great Global Warming. Butterfly lived with her pack that included the other Golden Fairywing butterflies, once only common in Samoa, as well as some Indigo Ladies (Greece), Goat-Mottled Tannenbaums (Madras) and the ornate Spider Butterflies (Croydon). Those warm December days were spent sipping at the nectar of the mango trees that lined Oxford Street, or chewing at the fruit of the luscious pawpaw bushes along the Strand.

Since the Warming, the commuters had cast off their dreary grey suits and ties, their dull pinafore dresses and sedate jackets. Instead they flocked into town like a feast of tropical parrots, riding the rails in open-topped trains, in bright hibiscus patterned shirts and pretty Fifties' frocks, sunglasses and sandals and tailored shorts and cotton tee shirts all the colours of every rainbow in the universe. Butterfly sometimes rode the rails with them, perched jauntily on someone's straw hat.

Since the Warming, people had got chatty. In the balmy Advent evenings, salsa bands played in Hanover Square, and strangers danced tangos into the night. Pimm's was quaffed down by the coral shores of the Thames, where the manatees begged for scraps of crackers and cheese and sometimes prawns tossed from the barbecues along the Embankment. Lovers strolled past cheery divers, just coming up from a good day's diving, happily discussing all the tropical fish they saw: the Madagascan Hawk Shrimp, the Caribbean Eel-Sharks and the Portly Sun-Fish.

No one worked for banks anymore; people produced things that were useful — surfboards and houses made of wood, decking for those warm evenings, carved dolphins for the fountains of Bexleyheath, sunhats and plastic forks for picnics, bright cotton bikinis and organic sun cream.

Butterfly loved to watch all this as she flitted from palm tree to nutmeg tree, eating all the things she wanted to eat. She and her special friends the Indigo Ladies sometimes camped out around the lianas dangling from the top of Nelson's Column, where they could see all the way to Worthing, home of the surfer. She had a very nice life and was a very happy butterfly.

But one day she woke up shivering. She looked out towards Worthing. It wasn't yellow and sunny in the dawn; it was white and glistening. Butterfly had never seen anything like this before. Her friend Colin the Red-Kneed Bandicoot told her that Ted the Lamb-Faced Skink had said that Samantha the Assyrian Vulture had flown over it and heard that the white stuff made you feel uncomfy; first with goosebumps, then with numbness, then with being dead. Butterfly didn't like the sound of it, but as long as it stayed in Worthing maybe everything would be alright.

But the next day the white glistening stuff had moved north to Haywards Heath. It was getting nearer. And although she still saw the yellow sun in the sky, it didn't warm her wings like it used to. Butterfly was worried. She felt uncomfy. Would this mean she would soon be goosebumply, then numb, then dead? During morning feeding time, her little wings felt heavy and cold as she attempted to flit butterfly-like from pawpaw to nutmeg bush. The uncomfy feeling became worse as the morning went on. Then at lunchtime her delicate legs shivered as she tried to balance on a mango, and, looking down, she saw that her lower half was covered in goosebumps. Because she admired the Stoics, she ignored the goosebumps and carried on trying to nibble through into the sweet mango flesh, but her little feet were so cold that she slipped off, and the mango went with her. Her wings felt crispy rather than fleet and, although she flapped them desperately, she knew she was fighting a losing battle. All she could do was to cling on to the mango as it was falling...falling...falling....

Butterfly woke up in the dark. She was warmer now, and she knew she wasn't outside. Her little toes were still clinging to the mango, and the mango was moving. Butterfly realised that she was sitting on top of the mango as it moved along, on what seemed to be a conveyor belt covered in sweet smelling meadow grass. Then she noticed something else, another smell, a warm kind of animal smell that wasn't nasty, but warm and thick and chewy. She heard munching and crunching, and then she realised where she was.

She was in the Stone Palace of the Cows, where cows were kept organically, safe and snug. The cows didn't like it too hot, so in the summer and winter they stayed in the cool stone courtyards and shaded Palace Meadows. The cows were happy cows because they kept their babies and there was still enough milk left over to make ice cream for the commuters at a reduced price. And because they were fed on the finest grass and the most beautiful wheat, the cows grew fat and contented. The only trouble with fat, contented cows, thought the people who looked after them, was the wind from their cow bottoms. So, because there had been rather a lot of methane and carbon dioxide to dispose of, the finest brains in all the land had collaborated to produce a neat little invention called the Deflatulator. The Deflatulator disposed of the excess gases by converting them into harmless candy floss, which was then distributed free to anyone who was hungry and fancied some candy floss.

But Butterfly didn't know about the Deflatulator as she rode the mango. She just knew that she felt much better, and, warming up with the cows' sweet breath, she stretched her wings and her little feet contentedly. This tiny stretchy movement made the mango unbalance ever so slightly, then pick up momentum and start rolling from side to side. And because mangos are a funny shape, neither spheroid nor ovoid nor squomboid or anything you can anticipate to any degree of accuracy, Butterfly couldn't work out which way to lean to keep the mango upright. And because fulcra had never been her strong point, even when she was a chrysalis and getting taught all that, she guessed wrongly. The mango overbalanced and toppled right into the northernmost cleft of the Deflatulator, taking Butterfly with it.

Butterfly could have given up there and then and, as a big fan of Epictetus, maybe she should have done and still been happy. But she liked paw paw, and her friend Colin the Bandicoot, and the Croydon Spider Butterflies, and sitting on hats. So, as she went spinning past the lip of the northernmost cleft of the Deflatulator, she stuck out her delicate leg and managed to hook a toe on. Pushing off with all her strength, Butterfly flew up, her magnificent wings outstretched and working to full capacity at last. She perched, breathless, on a flower woven into the fringe of a pretty Jersey cow and wondered what to do next.

As she sat and recovered, she sensed a deep vibration, and then she heard it. A low rumbling, a tumbling, a growing pressure of noise and steam seemed to build steadily from the cleft of the Deflatulator. If she had had gamma-ray vision like her friend Compton the Iguana, or perhaps a different kind of vision that could allow her to see through the special Deflatulator alloy that could only be manufactured in Gdansk, she would have seen that the mango had become wedged right in the heart of the machine. She could feel the revs increasing and knew something was up. She and the cows hurried over to the far side of the stone court to get out of the way and to see what would happen. They all realised that the Deflatulator's main flange was under strain, even the cows, and they had never had lessons in anything other than food hygiene. Then, the pressure became too much and, with a pink flash of sparkly delight, the Deflatulator exploded into a thousand and fourteen pieces, busting a heart-shaped hole through the roof, showering the cows with tasty candy floss and unleashing a tricubic dodekillion of special floaty rose-coloured carbon dioxide.

Up, up, up the carbon dioxide floated. The cows weren't bothered, they were too busy happily munching on the candy floss and licking it off each other's noses.

But Butterfly was bothered. She shook her wings free of the candy floss and slid down the Jersey Cow's nose, hoping that the Jersey Cow would lick away the sticky sweet residue that was crinkling her wings badly. The Jersey Cow was happy to and for good measure breathed on them to dry them off quickly. Butterfly was very grateful to the Jersey Cow because she wanted to see where the rosy cloud was going and she needed proper unsticky and dry wings for that. With her clean and dry wings Butterfly flew up through the heart-shaped hole in the roof. As she emerged into the sunshine, she could see the rosy cloud far above her, soaring upwards into the atmosphere. Even though she wasn't a betting butterfly, Butterfly would have wagered her precious wings that the rosy cloud would keep soaring up into the stars forever. But she was wrong — so she was pleased that she wasn't, in fact, a betting butterfly. Gradually the cloud slowed and spread out thinly, forming a huge pinkly-tinged haze, the shape, but obviously not the normal size, of a lady's sombrero.

As Butterfly found her bearings — she wasn't, in fact, very far from the mango tree she fell from— she could feel the temperature rising from decidedly chilly to a bit fresh to mild to balmy to pleasantly warm. It stopped at pleasantly warm. Then she realised why. The rosy mist was absorbing small chunks of infrared radiation, and sending them back down to warm the earth rather than along out to space. Butterfly flew back to Nelson's Column, and saw that the white glistening danger was melting back to where it came from, way, way down in the Antarctic. Soon it had disappeared and people in Worthing took off and aired their wellies.

Butterfly sat smiling and eating mango with her special friends the Indigo Ladies. She didn't know it, but she had saved her friends from a very chilly hundred thousand years. Another thing she didn't know was that the next week she would save her friends from the bloodthirsty hordes of Genghis Robinson, the second most feared warlord of the east.

Butterfly stretched her beautiful wings in the sunshine.

8 DR L. J. BARTLEY-DURWARD

Dr L. J. Bartley-Durward was thrown out of the Royal Society for Scientific Things Normal People Don't Understand because he had broken the golden rule. What the golden rule is has slipped my mind for a moment as I am writing this in hospital after particularly careless use of my third best sausage tongs. It's very difficult to hold a train of thought in hospital on a Saturday night after the pubs in Guildford kick out.

And because Dr Bartley-Durward was thrown out of the Royal Society for Scientific Things Normal People Don't Understand, he lost his funding and had to give up his laboratory to his rival, Professor Talgarth Flyover, the man that the president of the Royal Society for Scientific Things Normal People Don't Understand said would be the next Nobel prize winner, instead of Dr Bartley-Durward.

It hadn't always been this miserable for Dr Bartley-Durward. When he was a student at Cambridge University, his professors had predicted a brilliant future for him, because he possessed all the seven requirements of a great boffin:

1. Long, mad, wavy hair that he could tie back in a ponytail when he didn't want to dip it into his experiments. Sometimes he kept his hair loose because he did want to dip it into his experiments, as that was part of the experiment.
2. A brilliant mind.
3. Endless curiosity about everything.
4. A playful nature.
5. A slight speech impediment.
6. A grubby lab coat with ink coming through the breast pocket where his Biro had leaked.
7. Mild blue eyes that seemed to gaze off into the distance. This was especially disconcerting for his many friends who, seeing him lost in thought, asked him what he was pondering. They would expect him to say something world-shattering like, "Do you realise that if you bend the space-time continuum back on itself, everything would cease to exist in that place and reappear in exactly the opposite place? And I think I can prove it using only an egg timer and a bucket of kedgeree." But instead he would actually say something like, "Should I have honey or Marmite on my toast?" And then if one of his friends said something easy, such as "Would you like a crisp?" he would say, "I've just made a new element out of things I've found in the kitchen. I'm going to call it Porrigidium." So his friends could never be quite sure.

If you want to be a boffin, and a very good one, you need to have all seven of these requirements.

L. J. Bartley-Durward was christened Lawrence Jeremy by his proud and loving parents Stan and Ange Bartley-Durward, but everyone called him LJ. This is really handy for me because I don't have to keep on writing Dr L. J. Bartley-Durward or Lawrence Jeremy either.

LJ wasn't born of the loins of boffins. Boffindom wasn't thrust upon him. His boffinhood was made. His parents Stan and Ange didn't have a scientific bone in their bodies (except their actual bones) but they had endless curiosity, mad hair, playful natures and access to Explodo! Ltd, a chemistry set manufacturer, where Ange drove the forklift truck and Stan worked in accounts. The enlightened chairman of Explodo! loved his company's products, and his staff did too. So, to stop temptation, the Explodo! chairman let his staff have as many chemicals and reams of litmus paper as they wanted. A bit like at the Cadbury's factories, or is that an urban myth and I have been holding out for a career there in vain?

When toddler LJ showed no interest in the usual dull run of suspects of children's toys, Ange brought him a selection box of magnesium, lithium and sodium and a big bowl of water. From then on, LJ was hooked. Sometimes Ange brought him a tank of hydrogen and a box of matches. On days when Stan and Ange were up the allotment, LJ would mix up chlorine and milk – boom! Or dry ice and water – boom! Or toenail clippings and lemonade – nothing. That was a disappointing day. But most days, LJ found something to explode or foam or stink up the house with. He found that he loved playing with chemical elements, and the happier an element was, the more it played. He found that if you offered a chocolate to a piece of zinc, it would feel so happy that it would decide to react with water when normal, sad zinc wouldn't. If he watched a funny DVD with a slice of aluminium sitting on the floral sofa next to him, it would be too chilled to bother reacting vigorously to halogens, even the pretty ones, but it would melt for a laugh if you tickled it.

But LJ's favourite days were when Ange or Stan brought him things from the Explodo! Cupboard of Surprises, which contained packages of chemicals that had lost their labels, so no one knew what the chemicals were. Once he turned Rameses, next door's Bichon Frise, a fine primrose yellow with what LJ thought were strawberry bonbons but turned out to be something very different. The next month he managed to grow Rameses another head using some aromatic turquoise powder. His next-door neighbours were fine with it, because Rameses was a very handsome dog and another head was just something more to love about him. Rameses became fairly famous in the Batchester Argos as "Rameses, the Cuddly not-quite-Cerberus," and people used to come from at least a ten mile radius to pat him on his heads and give them treats.

At school, LJ confounded the teachers with questions they couldn't answer, like, "How can I make an inert gas ert?" The good teachers were overjoyed and said, "Good question! I have no idea. Let's try to find out." The rubbish teachers said, "Be quiet, Bartley-Durward, you are being insolent!" The scary teachers said, "Come into the stationery cupboard for a minute and I'll show you." But before he would do that he would be on to the next thing.

So LJ, being clever and boffiny, went up to Cambridge University — rather, he went down to Cambridge because he lived near Batchester, which is north of it — and he studied hard and everybody liked him. And because he was good at experiments, finding out new things and publishing interesting papers in the quality science journals that make universities pay a lot each year to subscribe to them, his head of department kept him on after graduating. Even better, he gave him funding so LJ didn't have to teach students or take tutorials in funny little rooms with wooden panels like in all the films where it's supposed to be Cambridge University. Instead, his head of department gave him a big laboratory full of glass things, smells, powders, liquids, granules of all colours and textures, slime, magnetic crunchy things and substances that you should never put in a baguette with cheese and tomato even if you are really, really hungry. His head of department told him to play in the laboratory on a daily basis and write down anything interesting that happened.

For five years LJ had a lovely time playing with chemicals alongside his faithful assistant Dr Colin Labcoat and his pet lab rat Tycho, whom Dr Colin had adopted from Bobchunks Lab Rat Rescue many years before. Tycho was blind in one eye and without a tail as someone had once tried to experiment on him but they had ended up badly mauled and with Weil's disease (Evil 0. Karma 1.), so in effect Tycho won on points.

Five years into his playing, during which he discovered lots of fascinating science things such as why stars are how they are and what happens if you liquidise solid gravity with a banana (this knowledge can never, ever be made public), LJ received some very sad news from home. He was busy in his laboratory when Dr Colin walked in.

"LJ, very sad news from home, I'm afraid," Dr Colin said. "Rameses the Bichon Frise has died. Obesity. It's having that second head. All those visitors, all those treats. And you know that the second head needed to be fed too or the heads would snap at each other. It's such a shame. He would have lasted a lot longer if he had been svelte under all that fluff. I'm ever so sorry."

LJ was devastated.

"I'm devastated," he said to Dr Colin.

"I'm devastated," he said to Ange and Stan when next he went home for Sunday lunch. He could see his next-door neighbours sitting on their patio, tears streaming down their faces and dripping off their chins as they gazed at the cherry sapling that marked Rameses' final resting place. LJ went out and put his head over the fence.

"Next-door neighbours, I'm so sorry. If I hadn't given him that second head, none of this would have happened."

Luckily, his next-door neighbours were gentle, kind people. They would sooner have sprinted naked into the street with a bunch of daffodils up their bottoms than phone Vexatious Litigance, top lawyer to the nation's greedy. You know the sort: "Been hurt? Not your fault? Not prepared to distinguish between just one of those things and negligence? Think life should be how you want it, all the time? Call Vexatious Litigance. No win, no fee, no scruples." Yuk.

"Rameses had a lovely life," his next-door neighbours said. "We don't regret his second head at all. If we had our time over again, we'd ask you to give him a third head, but we'd walk him more regularly. Please don't worry."

But LJ did worry. He worried a lot. He felt bad. Sometimes he dreamed of Rameses galloping through sunlit fields of poppies, his heads bobbing with pleasure, his tongues hanging out, all four of his eyes bright with the joy of life. But the affable porker-dog was dead and he would never again gambol through fields, even if he could have lumbered into more than a trot.

Back at the Lab, LJ realised he couldn't enjoy playing with molecules again until he had made it better for Rameses and his next-door neighbours. And the only way he could make it better was to go back in time and not give Rameses another head. Despite having invented many interesting things, such as the Microcombobulator, the Invisibilitator and the Regurgisludger, LJ had not yet invented his own time machine. So this became his broiling ambition.

"I have to do this. I have to make a time machine so everything will be alright again. I must command Time itself," LJ thought thoughtfully.

If you had heard someone other than LJ think, "I must command Time itself," you may have presumed they were one of the following types of people:

1 An Evil Baddy, whose ambition is to go back in

time and destroy good people before they did great things that confounded Evil.

2 A Heroic Goody, whose ambition is to go back in time and destroy evil people before they did bad things that confounded Good.

3 Me, who would like to go back to last Saturday morning to buy a lottery ticket containing all of the winning Lotto numbers plus the bonus number.

4 Dinophiles, who would like to go back to watch dinosaurs in real life, although this is flawed thinking as having a time machine doesn't stop you from smelling like lunch to a velociraptor.

But LJ was only doing it to make things better for his kind next-door neighbours and Rameses, the late Bichon Frise.

So, decision made, LJ rolled up his jumper sleeves and checked what he had in the laboratory cupboards. After he had made his selection of pink and green chemicals and a magnetic strinometer, he went to Homebase for some size 3.4mm twezzles and a gumbar holder. Then he took apart his old Victorian steampunk timepiece, removed the quartzite bungbung and three of the minty starters. He borrowed a set of sequential time dilators from the physics department and an egg and cress sandwich from the canteen. Then he bought a big box of Quality Street to keep the chemicals who weren't involved in the experiment happy. He was ready.

For days and long weeks LJ toiled in his laboratory. Contrary to his usual custom of letting anyone in to see what he was up to and to play with the chemicals alongside him, LJ banned everyone from his laboratory except for his loyal assistant Dr Colin and his lab rat Tycho.

The rest of the department pressed their noses up to the frosted internal windows, or peered under the doorframe. Sometimes they craned their heads over the shoulders of delivery men, who delivered supplies like packs of Westerhof's croziers, cases of tormaquite coagulants, which you can only get from the Dalmatian mountains in spring, and, once, a thin crust pizza with extra pineapple and olives. LJ preferred thin crust, as it helped him think; he had discovered this during the clay pizza shoot against the Department of Ancient Mnemonics the previous May. Stranger smells than usual, colours that hadn't quite existed before, foams and crystals that stuck to the windows; all these were a magnet for LJ's colleagues.

But as time went on, his colleagues became bored. Nothing except the smells and the foams seemed to be happening. So, one by one, over the days and weeks, they gave up and tootled back to their own laboratories where they did the boffin crosswords and pondered on their own experiments.

But one man stayed on to skulk around outside LJ's laboratory. This was Professor Talgarth Flyover, who was jealous of LJ's popularity and his brilliance. It wasn't as if Professor Flyover was stupid. Hadn't he received the Hurstmonslop Award for Sheer Cleverness twice in a row? Hadn't he collaborated with all the great scientists of the decade – Montmorency, Blenkinhov, De Huiper and Cody Schwarz III? Flyover even had a Magnitude 9 Pink Dwarf in the constellation Tiramisu named after him. But, like Salieri to LJ's Mozart, Prof Flyover realised he could never have the level of brilliance he so coveted.

One night, Professor Flyover could bear it no longer. He burned with curiosity to find out what LJ was working on. Shiftily he polished his glasses and waited for LJ and Colin to lock up for the night. As their footsteps faded away down the corridor, he took his chance. Creeping out stealthily (and shiftily, as before) from the shadows, he put his head to the door and listened. Silence. Using a Tesco's Clubcard and a clip stolen from his mother's Sunday hairpiece, he fiddled and faddled with the door lock just like in all the breaking-in scenes in movies you have ever seen. The door unlocked with a satisfying quack. Professor Flyover slipped in to LJ's lab and shut the door behind him.

In the half-light cast by a luminous binary dartboard that LJ had knitted the previous term, Flyover could see precisely nothing. That was because there was nothing to see, apart from the aforementioned dartboard. The room seemed totally empty. No lab benches, no bubbling liquids, no electronic gubbins, no flashing lasers, no blinking lights blink blink blink, nothing humming, nothing sparking. Nothing. Professor Flyover wandered around, his footsteps echoing across the space. He was known for his quick temper and his emotions could travel from calm to throwing a benny in under eight seconds. So his feelings climbed the emotional scales all the way up from puzzlement, frustration, irritation and resentment and were working their way towards a white-hot crossness when he felt something run up his leg. That something bit his kneecap hard. Professor Flyover yelled, and grabbed at the something. He missed. The something was very quick and shot further up his cords, up through his knickerleg and out the other side. As Professor Flyover flailed around, the something scuttled up his back, emerged from his jumper neck and bit him hard on the ear.

By this time Professor Flyover had run screaming from the room and was hurtling down the corridor towards the front door. As he ran he prised the something off his ear and looked at it. It was Tycho the Lab Rat. Professor Flyover had never respected life, having destroyed many of Tycho's relatives during experiments, and he didn't care about hurting Tycho. So, without even aiming carefully, he hurled Tycho across the corridor.

Professor Flyover was a tall man and Tycho was a small, half-blind rat, and the odds were just not fair. However, Tycho was lucky that Professor Flyover had a poor aim, as he landed in an open box of cheesy puffs, the type used for packaging, so he was more shocked and winded than hurt. But Professor Flyover felt the unwanted piercing that Tycho had given him and saw that Tycho was struggling a little for breath and being blind in one eye was a little disoriented. With one angry bound Flyover went to snatch up Tycho, who could only give out the most weak rat squeak. Intending in his wicked way to grab Tycho by the tail and dash his little rat brains out against the wall, Flyover was confounded with Tycho not actually having a tail. Not a man to give up easily where evil was concerned, Flyover thought he could manage much the same outcome using a hind leg as a centre of rotation. As he reached for Tycho, the little rat managed to get his breath back and, very frightened now, squealed for his life. The corridor lights boomed on and a voice spat out,

"Step away from the rat!"

It was LJ, breathing heavily and looking incensed. He was with Dr Colin, and they were returning to the lab with their pyjamas on and carrying a pizza for a night-time experiment. Dr Colin rushed forward and gathered up Tycho to safety, cuddling him close and soothing him with soft words and gentle strokes. LJ, who up until now has displayed for you a perfectly pleasant manner, had no idea himself of what he was capable now that his blood was up, but he was soon to find out. He walked up to Flyover and looked him square in his face.

"You tried to kill Tycho," he accused, and reached his hand up.

"Don't do it, LJ!" shouted Colin, anticipating him. "Think of your funding! Think of Rameses!"

But it was too late. LJ very slowly, very precisely took off Flyover's spectacles.

"You wouldn't…," gasped Flyover.

"Oh, but I would," said LJ calmly, as he held out the specs and snapped them cleanly in two. Then he dropped first one half, and then the other, on the floor and with his biker boot-slippers crunched them up until they were both just two little piles of fine dust and plastic pieces.

Flyover, blinking myopically and not looking so intelligent now, said, "You'll pay for this."

"A man of your calibre should be able to manage a more original phrase at this stage of the drama," said LJ, who went over to help to stroke Tycho, who was much calmer now and nibbling on an olive. Dr Colin looked concerned and whispered, "LJ, I'm concerned."

"You should be!" laughed Dr Flyover, "You've just broken the golden rule of the Royal Society for Scientific Things Normal People Don't Understand. Never break a fellow scientist's spectacles. (Author's note at this punctuationally-awkward place: this is the golden rule that had slipped my mind earlier.) You're finished. You're done for. You'll never work again."

And, sadly, so it mostly came to pass. With a heart heavier than a beef-in-ale pie with a lead-lined double crust, the Vice-Pro-Under Chancellor in Chief of Cambridge University had no option but to strip LJ of his funding, his laboratory and even his lab coat. Even Dr Colin was made to go to work for another scientist, Dr Rolf Bidawee, who, although a pleasant enough chap, wasn't as much fun as LJ. Some of this was because he studied fungus, mould and spores which were not Dr Colin's favourite things.

On his last day at Cambridge, LJ was sweeping the floor of his empty laboratory when Professor Flyover popped his head round the door in an evil manner.

"Where's your stuff? Where's all your equipment? Why is your lab empty? Where's the bubble chamber, the electromagniograph, the didactic aylesbury, the acetate bio-lampeter?"

"Oh, they're all here," said LJ, with a cryptic smile, "but good luck finding them." And then he left, in an extremely enigmatic way. His department stood back, heads bowed, very sad that they were losing a clever and nice scientist.

Stripped of his honours, LJ went back home to live with his mum and dad, Stan and Ange, who fed him cake and vegetarian sausages to keep his spirits up. Tycho the rat came to live with them as Dr Colin had to go on a sabbatical with Dr Bidawee to Grottlund, land of mould and scunge, and even Tycho didn't fancy that much.

Stan and Ange didn't see much of LJ. He spent days and days in the shed in the garden, locked in with Tycho, creating smells and foams and small explosions with things from the old Explodo! Cupboard of Surprises. Ange and Stan left plates of blancmange outside, and pots of Old Betty. One day LJ sent Tycho in to the house with a note tied to his foot. It read: Please drop Tycho outside the lab at Cambridge University, and wait for him. He will be carrying a small bag. Whatever you do, don't touch the bag.

What Stan and Ange didn't know and what no one in the world knew apart from LJ, Tycho the Rat and Dr Colin Labcoat and, oh yes, LJ's head of department and the faculty head and also some of LJ's ex-colleagues – but not Professor Flyover – was that while happily playing in the lab before Rameses died, LJ had invented the Microcombobulator, which made things very small, and the Invisibilitator, which made things fairly invisible. Actually, I think you know about these too as I mentioned them previously but if you haven't been paying attention then I draw them to your notice here. The Microcombobulator was invisible because LJ had put it in the Invisibilitator and the Invisibilitator was small because LJ had put it in the Microcombobulator. LJ had used the Microcombobulator and the Invisibilitator on all his laboratory equipment so it was now small and invisible, except the Invisibilitator, which was just small. All this made it quite difficult to find if one was to look for it.

So Stan and Ange drove to the parking bay outside the Lab. Tycho jumped out of the car, carrying a small cotton bag between his teeth. He scuttled into the building and twenty minutes later scuttled out again, the bag a different shape and obviously carrying things that weren't in it before. This was all LJ's lab equipment, which he needed to carry on making a time machine with.

"If LJ can't go to the Lab, then the Lab must come to LJ," thought Tycho, who was a very practical rat and a very excited one as LJ had said he could have the bag afterwards for nesting.

"Technically, this may be stealing," thought Stan and Ange, but didn't take it further as they felt LJ would give it back when he had finished with it.

The next day Stan and Ange had the next-door neighbours to afternoon tea on the lawn. LJ came out of the shed, covered in a fine layer of pink ash, and said, "Ooh, Mum, is there enough for me?" His eyes were shining and bright, and he had his smile back.

"Of course, love!" Ange was so pleased to see LJ happy again.

Over a dish of local speciality Abigail's Tansy and a strong pot of Old Betty, the neighbours outlined a plan for a memorial statue to Rameses to be erected in Batchester town centre during the Mayor's Summer Slug Balancing Festival that June.

"You won't need a statue," said LJ. "Just wait. I'm nearly there."

"But Rameses is dead and nothing can bring him back," said his next-door neighbours. "We really have gone through this before. We don't hold you responsible. As a scientist your memory should be better. Don't let remorse drive you more bonkers than you already are."

LJ thought hard. Tycho nibbled on a piece of Abigail's Tansy.

"If I can get Rameses back for you, would that make you happy?"

"More than anything in the world," his next-door neighbours said. "But how are you going to do that?"

"I just need one final piece of the jigsaw," LJ muttered, in a distracted-scientist kind of way.

"Which piece have you lost, darling?" asked Ange, his mum. "I found a piece of jigsaw under the hydrangea. It's either a piece of sky with a bit of cloud on it, or a basket/kitten fur interface. I can't remember. Look, here it is, it's in my bag," she said, taking something out of her Trojan haversack. "Oh, it's the basket/kitten fur interface!"

"I was speaking metaphorically, Mum," said LJ, "but I think you have given me exactly what I need. I've been looking for a small, oddly-shaped piece of cardboard. One side must be printed in colour with a glossy texture, the other side needs to be plain. It's to act as a solid-fill refractant for the second dichroic merganser, which you know isn't regular, so this'll do nicely." He took the jigsaw piece, planted a smacker on his mum's cheek, and with a cheery wave to the neighbours went skipping back to his shed.

After two days and two nights of solid work, stopping only for six meals, several snacks and two good nights' sleeps as well as a trip to the Bell and Badger with Stan his dad to watch the squirrel wrestling, LJ at last finished the time machine. He stood back and admired his handiwork. Tycho sat on his shoulder, admiring it too, especially the perfect ratbite holes in the casing for the string; the rat bites that Tycho had provided to help LJ complete his work that melded science and art.

The time machine was beautiful. If you can imagine the offspring of a sprint wheelchair and a Soviet-made anti-tank gun from the 1950s, soldered at the centre point with a set of hotwired pogo sticks, angled to allow for a cut-in section for the ion drive and a bentwood nosecone sculpted to reduce drag, then you have an excellent imagination. The machine didn't look like that at all. It looked like an ancient milk float with no roof, no wheels, no bonnet and no engine. Instead, it had stirrups for the driver's feet, an upturned bucket for the driver to sit on and a pulsating, glowing orb of controlled ectoplasm hovering above the chassis. It was perfect.

The next day dawned bright and clear. "A wonderful day for time travel," thought LJ. He ate a hearty breakfast then walked down the garden path to the shed, with Tycho scuttling after him.

LJ settled on the bucket and put his feet in the stirrups. He set the co-ordinates to fifteen years before, the day he had given Rameses a second head. Don't forget that in this story dogs live upwards of 40 years, so Rameses dead at 20 was too young. Yes, alright, I made a mistake with the timing of this one. But never mind that, LJ took a last look at the shed curtain, which was his focal point for time measurement. Fifteen years before, the curtains had been made from a sprightly pink Madras silk weave, but after an unfortunate explosion involving salad cream which, as you all know, is, like dribble, a devil to get out of silk, Stan had replaced them with an early Cath Kidston sprigged cotton.

LJ grasped the glowing orb of ectoplasm with both hands and said, "Tycho, throw the switch."

Tycho, waiting with twitchy-nosed anticipation, his eyes bright and his tail stub flicking excitedly, did precisely nothing.

"Tycho, the switch," repeated LJ. Tycho twigged what he was supposed to do, and pulled the switch.

In one blinding flash, LJ realised that nothing had happened. The curtains were still Cath Kidston. He was still in the shed today and not in the shed fifteen years before. He heaved a disappointed sigh, and Tycho's ears drooped. But before LJ could dismount from the bucket and check the connections, a voice said, "Well, this isn't Osgood Thoroughby."

LJ and Tycho turned to see that a little middle-aged lady had appeared in the corner of the shed, looking bemused and somewhat interested in the proceedings. She carried an embroidered hessian bag, wore sensible shoes and had a spider tattoo on her neck. A waft of warm hoof pasty accompanied her.

"Who are you?" asked LJ then, remembering his manners, said, "but do sit down and let me get you a cup of Old Betty."

"My name is Gladys," said Aunt Gladys, for it was she (and if you are unsure of who Aunt Gladys is, go back and read Aunt Gladys Fails to Return for she is in it, as the title might suggest), "and I'm on my way to pick up my little nephew whom I've left waiting at St Linoleum's. I've left him at the graveyard and it's lunchtime, although those two things are not related. He must be getting worried. What year is it?"

"By my watch," said LJ, peering at his second best My Little Pony wristwatch, "it's 18 years later than where you were previously."

"Goodness!" said Gladys, "I'm late. But a cup of Old Betty would go down nicely as I try to puzzle out how on earth I got here." Tycho twinkled off to mime to Ange to put the kettle on.

LJ said, "I'm so pleased to meet you, not just because you seem to have a warm personality which is always a joy. It means that my time machine is at least working. But although your presence is a delight, having you here doesn't help my situation," and he outlined in less than seventeen sentences the main thrust of the story so far, including the plot architecture, his own character arc and a brief description of all the main dramatic personae.

"And so I need me back there, not you here, so I can save Rameses from an early and portly grave," he concluded.

Aunt Gladys said, "I would love to help you but I shouldn't be in this story. I'm worried about my nephew waiting at the church, for good reason. There is an ancient curse upon my family, handed down to us from the Scunthorpian Oracle, and I quote: "Should a Scarabond remain waiting at a church for 18 years, then they shall be smited by the love of a beautiful woman." You can see that there is danger for him."

"Is smited a word?"

"I believe so."

"Smited with what?"

"The love of a beautiful woman."

"He will be destroyed by the love of a beautiful woman?"

"Indeed."

LJ thought a little and then said, "Are you sure it's not smitten? Smitten with a love for a beautiful woman?"

Aunt Gladys paused. "That would make more sense," she conceded.

"So if your nephew waits at a church for more than 18 years he will be smitten with love for a beautiful woman."

"Yes, that sums it up."

"And if he doesn't wait at a church for 18 years, the chances are he'd probably be smitten with love for a beautiful woman anyway."

Aunt Gladys considered this. "You know, perhaps I should have gone back to the original Greek on this one; my sister Jean was never a solid classicist. You're probably right. There's no danger."

She opened her bag and offered him a still-warm hoof pasty.

"No thanks," smiled LJ, "I'm vegetarian."

"These are vegetarian. In fact, they are vegan."

"In that case, yes please, that would be lovely. Would you like a sandwich? Since I was kicked out of the Royal Society for Scientific Things Normal People Don't Understand and Cambridge University, my dad has made a packed lunch for me every workday. Let's see, what do we have today?" He opened a large sandwich box and handed Aunt Gladys a menu. Aunt Gladys read:

Menu du jour
Deux sandwiches du fromage et pickle aussi
Un sandwiche oeuf mayonnaise (hold the gherkin)
Un sac du crisps (ready salted)
Un Pingouin

"My dad is learning French," explained LJ, "and he likes lunch to be an ocassion."

"Did you realise you said ocassion?"

"Did I? I'm so sorry, I meant occasion. I just can't seem to think straight. It's this experiment. It seems to have worked one way, that's why you're here, but I just can't get it to go backwards. Sometimes one can be too close to one's creation. I need someone to check the blueprints."

Tycho reappeared pushing a small trolley with a pot of Old Betty and three cups.

"Perhaps the problem is minor. For a start, have you checked the connections?" asked Aunt Gladys, as she perused the lungiform straddlers which occupied the main flange of the oblators around the time machine's casing. LJ checked the connections.

"They're all fine," said LJ, "thank you for being so practical."

"Yes, I'm very practical, hence these sensible shoes, but I don't have vision. What we need is someone who can visualise the whole thing and tell you where you've gone wrong."

"Yes, that's exactly what we need," agreed LJ, "but I don't think I know anyone like that. Let's tuck in to lunch and think about it."

While they were eating their lunch, which was a trifle early but no one was complaining, and musing on the problem, they heard a strange noise: a tap, tap, tapping. It was soft at first, but grew more distinct and louder as it travelled up the garden path toward the shed.

Tap…tap…tap.

"Is that the tap?" asked Aunt Gladys.

"No, that would be more of a drip, drip, drip," said LJ.

Tap...tap...tap…. The tapping got closer and closer but before they could place their sandwiches and pasty down in a clean area to get up to investigate, a quiet, well-educated voice said, "Is that hoof pasty I can smell?"

The door creaked open and round it came a white stick, followed by two skinny legs and the rest of an extraordinary person; a man whose face was golden and wrinkled with long years of exotic climates without sunscreen and whose far-seeing misty eyes — which LJ and Aunt Gladys could not yet see because they were hidden beneath dark glasses — were hidden beneath dark glasses (told you). He had long matted grey hair, active, gnarled fingers and he wore a ragged frock coat on top of a swathe of patched linen which was wrapped around his loins, a fashion almost unheard of in the Batchester area. His weathered feet were attached to a pair of ancient battered flip-flops, and he carried a big bag of pencils. The man stopped, uncertain.

"Good morning," said LJ, slightly fazed by not one but two polite strangers in his shed. "Do please sit down."

The man hesitated. "Oh, I would love to, but perhaps you could help me to a seat?"

LJ suddenly realised the man was blind.

"Gosh, I'm so sorry! The white stick was a giveaway. I should have been more considerate," he said, getting up to guide the gentleman — for they were both sure that the man, despite his strange attire, was a gentleman — to the seat next to Aunt Gladys.

"Pardon me, no offence at all," said the man. "A white stick is not necessarily an indication of blindness. During my sojourn in the easternmost reaches of Mbantogogogoch all the men of the Umvimto tribe carried white sticks as a sign of virility and as a visual reminder to put the bins out on Thursdays. But you're right, I am blind, and have been ever since I retired from work."

Aunt Gladys looked puzzled. "I'm sorry for this question, but if you are blind, why the dark glasses? Isn't that cheating?"

"The government is after me," whispered the man, "so while I am back in the country I must disguise myself."

"But what are you disguised as?" asked LJ, quite at a

loss at the combination of loin cloth, frock coat and flip-flops.

"Ah, that's my problem, there have been so many options and I could never decide. I'm just going with it, at the moment."

"What did you do before you retired?" asked Aunt Gladys, offering the stranger half a hoof pasty and the end of a cheese and pickle sandwich.

"I was a town planner," said the stranger.

"Gosh, how did you cope being in competition with Dave, the town planners' town planner?" asked LJ.

Now, dear reader, if you are the methodical type and are reading Happy Stories for Busy People in the right order, you would have read How Magnus Southeby Was Built and already met Dave. However, if you are one of these mad-as-a-gussetful-of-woodlice types and take pleasure in throwing caution to the winds by reading a book of short stories in the wrong order and have therefore not yet read How Magnus Southeby Was Built, meet Dave now. Dave is a brilliant town planner who was very famous and disappeared mysteriously many years ago. But do go back and read How Magnus Southeby Was Built because I'm quite pleased with it. But not yet, finish this story first. But remember, LJ and Aunt Gladys don't know that the stranger is Dave yet.

LJ continued, "Dave was extraordinary. Many apologies for being so effusive about a competitor, but his work was so exciting. He was a true visionary. I named one of my early inventions after one of his early towns. Gladys, do you remember the beautiful stone-cladded swans at Gravelly St Gerard?"

"Works of art," agreed Gladys, "and after the majesty of Magnus Southeby he mysteriously disappeared. The papers say he is dead. It's such a shame."

The stranger paused and then said, "The papers are mistaken."

"Lordy! Do you know what happened to him? Is he alright? Do you know where he is?" asked LJ.

"Indeed I do," said Dave, for, guess what, it was he, as you already know.

"I am he," he confirmed.

LJ, Aunt Gladys and Tycho all gasped with wonder and pleasure. Dave, the town planner, whom all had feared dead (a rumour with no substance) had come back from the grave (where he had never been) and returned full of life (despite having never been dead) to the land he had disappeared from all those years ago. It was a holy blessing for future towns, a thumb in the armpit for secret men in the government who disapprove of habitable towns, and very good for this story too, as Dave is about to provide the solution that will create a happy ending that you have been waiting in vain for all this time, while no doubt drumming your fingers impatiently on the innocent commuter to your left or your imperious cat Bowser.

Aunt Gladys said, "One of my cousins lives in Magnus Southeby. She's a black belt in literacy at the Library Fight Club. She adores it there."

"Yes," said LJ, "we nearly moved there when Explodo! opened a new factory on the outskirts, but the town was so popular it was full up."

"I have missed this country," said Dave. "It's amazing how much better one's mind works when cooped up indoors when it is raining and freezing out. During my travels it was so sunny and hot, all I did was bathe in beautiful clear waters, sunbathe on golden sands and eat pineapple. Locals gave me alms and once, arms, with which I used to shoot down more pineapple, which was a challenge for bystanders given that I can't see. Even though I had my bag of pencils with me at all times, my brain was so blissed out that it lost its avocado of creativity. I need another challenge. I just couldn't stay away any longer."

LJ mused while Tycho poured out a second cup of Old Betty for Aunt Gladys and LJ, and a first for Dave. Tycho, who was a very kind rat, had given up his cup to

Dave and was content to sip out of Aunt Gladys' saucer.

"Dave," said LJ, "I know your speciality is towns, but how are you on time machines?"

"I'm not bad," said Dave. "When I designed Lordly Underpenny, I placed a few small time bouncy castles in the children's centre and three of the pubs."

"So that's why the children and drunks of Lordly Underpenny are considered such liars! All those stories of discussing religion with Hilda of Whitby or fleeing the Black Death at Harmonious Blacksmith. Now it all makes sense!" said LJ.

"Do you have the blueprint for the time machine?" asked Dave. "I feel rested and able to contribute to the action of this story and bring it to a gentle conclusion."

"Yes, it's over there," said LJ, pointing to the luminous knitted binary dartboard hanging up by the Take That poster, the luminous knitted binary dartboard that Tycho had taken from the university laboratory alongside the rest of LJ's lab equipment. Aunt Gladys helped Dave over to it, and he ran his hands up and down the weave.

"Ah, I can see immediately what your problem is," said Dave. "Your cabling is the wrong way round. See, it should be left crossing not right crossing. You should have brought the needle to the front of the work."

"So that's why I brought Aunt Gladys from the past into the present, rather than me back to the past," said LJ.

"What vision you have, Dave!" remarked Aunt Gladys, her face lit up with a strange rosy glow that was nothing to do with hot flushes. She went on, "LJ, I can see that you've dropped a stitch in the thirteenth row, and you've purled where you should have knitted in the 5th row, next to 1011. That's why your place co-ordinates are 5 degrees of arc off."

"What a grasp of detail you have, Gladys!" remarked Dave, his face lit up with a strange rosy glow, which was nothing to do with sunburn.

"So all I have to do to make the time machine work,"

said LJ "is knit up the blueprints correctly."

So Aunt Gladys held the luminous wool (made of Lumolin™, which LJ had invented when he had looked after a woolly ewe and an ultra-violet ray gun for a friend) while LJ unwound the wrong bit and knitted it back up correctly. It did take most of the afternoon so LJ's dad Stan took Dave to visit Batchester's Pantheon, modelled on Dave's great construction at Bourton-on-the-Waterslide.

When the blueprint was corrected and the time machine changed accordingly — it only needed an extra flange paddler angled into the bucket and one more minty starter— LJ was ready to go and sort out Rameses, the late two-headed dog. Dave, Aunt Gladys and Tycho stood back to watch.

"What's your plan?" asked Dave.

"I'm going to go back to the hour before I grew Rameses a second head, and then not do it."

"Why don't you go back further and bring him back as a puppy, then your lovely next-door neighbours could have him for longer?" suggested Aunt Gladys.

"What a good idea," said LJ. "Why didn't I think of that?"

"Typical aunt's logic," said Dave, winking from behind his dark glasses at where he thought Aunt Gladys was. Aunt Gladys chuckled manfully and took his hand, which made him jump as he thought she was 70 degrees and five feet east of him (which would have put her in the flowerbed outside), which was incorrect.

"Tycho," said LJ, "please throw the switch."

Tycho, quivering with a ratful of excitement, threw the switch.

Immediately everyone knew it had worked because there was a flash, a crash, the curtains flew up, the door flew open and the time machine moved one and a half feet to the west. There was a happy-puppy-barking sound and LJ, now wearing a pink floral sundress, stepped out of the machine. He was clutching a very wriggly, very fluffly, very happy and very one-headed puppy Rameses.

"I landed in a washing line," explained LJ about the frock, "and I've also brought back the turquoise aromatic powder, because I want to find out just how it grows second heads."

LJ held an unmarked plastic bottle, but before he could place it or Rameses down to get on with the next stage of his life, finish this story and to make his next-door neighbours happy, a dark shadow wearing cords and new glasses raced in, grabbed the turquoise aromatic powder and ran off again, shouting, "At last, I have confounded you, LJ! I have your turquoise aromatic powder, and you'll never get it back!" It was Professor Talgarth Flyover who, on his day off, had decided to steal something of LJ's to really annoy him.

LJ shrugged his shoulders. "I'm not that bothered about the powder. He's welcome to it. After all, I have a time machine and I have Rameses back."

I can't describe to you the scene when LJ reunited Rameses with his kind next-door neighbours, because I wasn't there. But if I was I am sure my careworn eyes would have been too full of happy tears to be able to take in the details and report them back to you accurately. I am sure that it was a joyous occasion. I did hear that Mr next-door neighbour was very pleased to get his pink sun frock back, as that had cleared up another mystery.

Another joyous occasion was the wedding of Aunt Gladys and Dave, with Aunt Gladys' one-handed nephew, found through wise use of the time machine, as giver-away-of-aunt and with Rameses as chief bridesdog. The wedding was celebrated at St Truelove's at Cranberry Magnificence, Dave's second favourite town. At Cambridge, Professor Talgarth Flyover accidentally gave himself another head with the turquoise aromatic powder and became very popular on science chat shows and in laboratories around the world. He became very happy at his celebrity, and so he sat down and wrote a letter to LJ saying how sorry he was about everything and would he like his old job back at Cambridge University, and be president of the Royal Society for Scientific Things that Normal People Don't Understand, as he (Flyover) was sure he (Flyover) could swing it for him (LJ).

As for LJ, he took his old job back and brought Dr Colin Labcoat back from Grottlund, and LJ, Dr Colin and Tycho had many adventures in the time machine, adventures I couldn't possibly relate here as some of them are frankly terrifying and terrifying adventures have no place in a book of happy stories. Look for them in The Book of Terrifying Adventures and Other Charming Pastoral Tales.

LOUISE SAYS STUFF HERE

I do hope you liked my stories. If you did, please tell me and everyone else, too. If you didn't then shhh!! Let's just keep it between you and me.

I am normally a poet because I like words such as "meander", "cor blimey" and "lederhosen", so if you are feeling strange then go take a look at my poems online or my collections *Slightly Wrong* and *More Slightly Wrong*, from Waterstones or Amazon, in real paperback or more tenuous e-book. I always bow down to jolly emails from people who read my stuff so if you have nothing better to do today, then say hello at louise@louiseetheridge.com

Website: http://www.louiseetheridge.com
Twitter: @LouEtheridge
Facebook: www.facebook.com/LouiseDoesWords
.

www.ingramcontent.com/pod-product-compliance
Lightning Source LLC
Chambersburg PA
CBHW021935040426
42448CB00008B/1081